Special Words

NOTES FOR WHEN YOU DON'T KNOW WHAT TO SAY

Joyce Landorf Heatherley

MOORINGS
Nashville, Tennessee
A Division of the Ballantine Publishing Group,
Random House, Inc.

All Scripture quotations, unless otherwise indicated, are from THE LIVING BIBLE (Wheaton, Illinois: Tyndale House Publishers, 1971) and are used by permission.

Scripture quotations marked (NIV) are from the HOLY BIBLE, NEW INTERNATIONAL VERSION®. Copyright © 1973, 1978, 1984 by International Bible Society. Used by permission of Zondervan Bible Publishing House. All rights reserved.

The "NIV" and "New International Version" trademarks are registered in the United States Patent and Trademark Office by International Bible Society. Use of either trademark requires the permission of International Bible Society.

Scripture quotations marked (KJV) are from The Holy Bible, KING JAMES VERSION.

Scripture quotations marked (TEV) are from TODAY'S ENGLISH VERSION—Old Testament: Copyright © American Bible Society 1976, 1992, New Testament: Copyright © American Bible Society 1966, 1971, 1976, 1992. Used by permission.

Library of Congress Cataloging-in-Publication Data

Heatherley, Joyce Landorf.
    Special words : notes for when you don't know what to say / by Joyce Landorf Heatherley.
        p.   cm.
    ISBN: 0-345-40301-0 (hardcover)
    1. Letter writing.   2. Social stationery.   3. Heatherley, Joyce Landorf.   I. Title.
    BJ2101.H43   1996
    395'.4—dc20   95-51542
                                                                CIP

First Edition: March 1996

10   9   8   7   6

This book is dedicated to the cherished memory of my
infant son

David Andrew Landorf

December 31, 1964

Contents

CONTENTS

Acknowledgments

My dear Readers,

One person may *write* a book, but it takes a multitude of people and lots of hard work to *make* a book. This book is no different, so it's highly appropriate that I write the following words. They are from my heart.

I'm grateful to the staff at Moorings, Connie Giles, my "in-house" editor, and Linda Thomsen, my administrative assistant.

Finally, I'm grateful to the dear people in my life . . . you know exactly who you are . . . for your spoken or written words that have continually flooded my heart with a sea of loving support.

I am grateful. Deeply grateful!

Love,

Joyce

Introduction

My dear Reader,

As I look back over my years of writing—beginning in adolescence with my laboriously handwritten thank-you notes to grandparents, aunts, and other family members and later on to magazine articles, columns, and eventually to many manuscripts both published and unpublished—a surprising and satisfying truth emerges.

And it's this: Of all the ways to communicate with another human being, it is not writing the great American novel but rather the little, pristine gem called the handwritten note that touches our hearts the most. It's that small missive of love and hope that—whether we write it or receive it—has the remarkable power to transform our state of mind and alter our emotions through a precious, soul-gratifying experience. Even in sad or disturbing circumstances, the handwritten note is deeply personal, sometimes moving.

When a handwritten note comes into our day, it lifts

our spirits, tickles us into a smile or a laugh, revives a milieu of memories, announces some good or bad news, or informs us about an event or experience—and for a short span of time, we are held captive by its effects. Ours is a truly wonderful world for written communiqués— handwritten or computerized, mailed or faxed. The main point I want to make in this book is simply this: I want to encourage you to write out (by *whatever* means) your heartfelt thoughts and ideas. Write them down on something, and send them to the person of your choice. Use either or any method—just do it.

Personally, I love the delicate ambiance of the handwritten notes and letters, so this is my bias. But even as I write these words, I can hear in my head all the CCL (completely computer literate) people in my life—even grandkids—shouting, "Excuse me? Handwritten notes in this age of computers?" Or, "Grandma Joyce, get with it! We're in Computer Country now. Even first graders know that a mouse is not some furry little animal in 'Hickory Dickory Dock' who runs up the nursery rhyme clock!"

Okay, I know their admonitions are all true. We do live in the wonderful age of computers, faxes, answering machines, mobile phones, and personal beepers, and I certainly don't mean to exclude computer-aided writing— nor do I want to imply that a message *not* written by hand is impersonal and can't be effective. It definitely can touch the heart. Maybe my preference is due in part to the fact that, as a music major, I couldn't see any sense in taking a typing class in high school or college. To this day,

I cannot understand even the simplest computer instructions. Each of the twenty-four books I've written, including this one, has been written out (several times) in longhand—one of my peculiar idiosyncrasies. Also, for me, typing and computers move at too great a speed for my mind to keep up. I think better with the slow-paced flow of the ink from my pen. Or—perhaps I'm just getting old and set in my ways!

At any rate, to motivate you to write out your notes, here are some reasons to explore the beauty of writing notes by hand.

First, unlike those generated by computer, handwritten notes become very personal. Between the scaled-down size of the stationery and your handwriting, your note announces that it is not an advertisement, a business letter, an innocuous form letter, or junk mail addressed to "occupant." And when people see your individualistic handwriting, they glimpse a very special part of your personality, far more than they would see from just your signed name (even if you've been accused of being a doctor because your handwriting is so illegible!).

A few years after C. S. Lewis's death, I had a personal conversation with Walter Hooper, who had become the great scholar's official literary executor. Walter recounted the fact that Lewis was once asked why he continued to handwrite all his correspondence when the volume of mail kept escalating each time he wrote another book, especially after his hands were deeply affected by the pain and crippling effects of arthritis. Lewis's profound answer was, "I write in my own hand because of the worth of the human soul [who wrote to me]."

I believe that when we get a handwritten note in this, the age of computers, we tend to catch our breath, sit down, and take the message. Don't ask me *why* this happens, I just know it does.

A second reason for writing notes is this: We all know that everything in this world takes time. But putting a few well-chosen words down on paper and sending it to someone tends to get his or her attention, reaches the heart of the subject matter quickly, and goes a long way toward *saving* time, after all. I believe that notes "reach out and touch" people in a better way than the phone company advertises—perhaps because the recipient of the note doesn't have to respond immediately but can reflect on the written words privately.

Here's a third reason for you to consider: I don't think for one single second that published writers like myself have the market cornered on stringing words together to convey the joy or the sorrow of the moment. Years of receiving notes from people all over the world have convinced me. Those handwritten missives from nonprofessional writers run the gamut from cute, amusing, and clever to articulate, sincere, and even profound. In fact, many thoughts written by "nonwriters" are among the most comprehensible and articulate I've ever read. But maybe if you don't *think* you know how to write, you just need a nudge here and there, so you might want to think of these pages as a "nudge" book. I've provided many letters and notes on a variety of real-life topics that I hope will give that nudge to you in the same way cue cards or 3 × 5 inch cards prompt a speaker.

These examples have been inspired by thirty-five years of correspondence and conversations with the thousands of people I've encountered during my public and professional life.

All these years of writing books and speaking engagements have given me the delightful opportunity to "listen between the words" and to "take the pulse" of my readers and of the people in my audiences. So this book is not merely a collection of generic model letters but is a compilation of personal responses to very personal experiences and situations. They are totally fictionalized in terms of connections to particular individuals but are intensely true to the ways I have experienced and observed life to be.

Read the simple lines offered in this book, and who knows, you may feel a wave of inspiration, change your viewpoint, or gain a new perspective. Then, so armed (and without fear of copyright infringement!), you can tailor-make these notes using your own pet phrases or personal illustrations that will add the "sound" of your voice to your writing. Perhaps these pages of prompters may even awaken the dormant gift of writing within you—a gift that may have been sleeping or hiding way down in your soul. This is especially likely if you are thinking, *I know I should write a note, and I want to write, but I just don't know where to start or what to say.*

In the past year as I've been dealing with biopsies, surgeries, tests, chemotherapy, and all that goes with breast cancer, it's been the avalanche of handwritten notes from people (only a few of them authors or practicing writers) that have showered my daily existence with tiny waterfalls of exquisite joy. Those notes have brought moments of much-needed relief from the relentless pressures of dealing with cancer. In the seconds it took me to read those notes filled with expressions of love, offerings of hope, and spoonfuls of encouragement, I was enabled somehow to set aside a few of the monumental horrors like nausea, fatigue, setbacks, and long waits in doctors' offices for treatments or lab results. The notes were interludes — brief but beautiful.

So, with great affection I say, when you can't find the words or you don't have an idea in the world about how to start a note (especially if you're struggling because it's a difficult subject), then read through these pages. Pick and choose; reject or accept; revise, add, delete — whatever. But find the note or letter that prompts you to write out of your heart in the very best way possible. Let it propel you, motivate you, into the almost-forgotten realm of enhancing relationships by means of your special, personal handwritten note. Experience the rewarding joy of writing.

Love,
Joyce

Special Words
for Special Days

∽

My dear Reader,

You know, we are really blessed with the availability of an abundant variety of greeting cards in the marketplace. All through the year, for every occasion, we can buy a card that fits someone perfectly. And now there are even those beautifully pictured blank cards (my favorites).

But even when I receive a beautiful, humorous, or to-the-heart-of-the-matter card, I always look for the sender's handwritten note at the bottom or on the back. And I feel disappointed when the card is merely signed— or worse, there's no signature, only an imprint. I cherish the scribbled words from loved ones no matter how timely the card is, because somehow those few words personalize it and warm my heart with a graceful, caring touch that means a great deal.

When my children were growing up, they usually

bought cards for our family's birthdays and other special occasions at our home, but they also knew that I'd insist on a note or a letter tucked inside the card. What they didn't know was that I would save all those cards and notes, box them, and then give them back to them on their fortieth birthdays. Seeing their surprise and then their joy as they opened those boxes of notes and cards has to rank right up there as one of my finest hours as a mother. I'll never forget the thrill.

Add your thoughts to each card you send, or enclose a letter of love. It's an outstanding and important way to communicate from the heart.

Love,

Joyce

Birthday

My dear Mary Ellen,

It's your birthday today! Angels clapped their hands in joy the moment your mom heard your first cry—and we who love you have continued the applause!

Enclosed is a rose sachet I made for you . . . from my garden. I send it to you as I know how very difficult this past year has been for you.

Sometimes when my own pain is great and it even hurts to take a breath, the fragrance of the roses in my garden carries me to a safe place.

I pray it does the same for you in this, a brand-new year of your life!

Happy birthday, dear one.

> Love,
> Your cousin

Birthday

Dearest Margaret,

I know you love tulips like I do. I think we both inherited that love from our moms.

Today I wrote this poem after thinking about you, your upcoming birthday on the twelfth of this month, and your love of tulips.

> The tulip said —
> It's winter, dark and cold down here.
> I'm put away, buried under a mountain
> I'll never bloom for your Glory
> so what are you doing to me,
> Lord?
>
> The Lord answered — I've placed you
> exactly where it's best for you.
>
> I know
> just how much you can bear and I'll unfurl
> your fragile petals for the world to see.

But for now, dear tulip,
trust and obey me.

So dear one, may your birthday bring with it—the special excitement of knowing everything he has planned for you is definitely right on schedule.

Happy Birthday!

You are loved,

Birthday

Dearest Grace,

I bought this humorous card because it made me laugh *and* think of us—two old, old, old friends. And I hope it makes you laugh as well. (A real knee-slapper, as they say.)

But along with the laughter this card brings, I just want to be serious for a moment and tell you:

All these years I've been grateful for every birthday you and I have had—but none so much as each new one.

Cancer may well shorten the years in the future, but cancer can't stop either of us from cheering wildly when it's time to celebrate *another* year together!

Hooray for this day!

Love,

Birthday

Dearest Mary,

Your birthday without Ellen, your twin sister, must feel like the last nail pounded into your emotions. To be separated for any length of time was difficult when Ellen was here—but it must be enormously difficult now . . . especially on your birthdays. Celebrating is a mixed bag.

I grew up as an only child, so I don't have any idea of how strong twins' connecting tissues can be. I do remember the delightful ambiance of joy that always surrounded you two, especially as children. If you fought, argued, or disagreed about things, I have to commend you on the fact that you surely never let any of us hear it or see it. (Although, if you *did* have a difference of opinion, I'm sure your mom and dad knew it . . . but not your friends or others!)

Today I wish you a happy birthday, and I also wish happy memories to flood over you. I'll be thinking of all the times I was a part of those memories as well.

My love,

Birthday

Dearest Son,

I remember the first moment I saw you. (Boy, do I *remember*!) I can still see your sleepy eyes opening wide (gorgeous blue) and hear your vigorous cry. Even the nurses said how beautiful you were. Maybe they said that to all the new mothers, but I took it personally! And I still do. (I also remember, when you were just a year old, a clerk in a store took a good look at you and exclaimed, "Oh, my! He's got *bedroom eyes*!" What could I say?)

The other day, as I watched your love and pride shine through your face as you talked to *my* grandchildren, I recalled that first time I saw you in the hospital some forty years ago, and I thought, "My, he hasn't changed a bit! He's still beautiful!"

Happy birthday, Son!

Lovingly,
Mom

Birthday

My dearest Jon,

You were a brand-spanking-new six-weeks-old when God and your birth mother gave us our first look at you.

My, how we prayed for one more child to add to your

sisters—but as you know, all our efforts to adopt fell through again and again. I'd almost given up hope. But then your father came rushing home one day shouting the news.

"Guess what! I got *the* call today, and it looks good! We're going to be able to adopt a baby boy! The paperwork isn't completed, but most of the details have been cleared and taken care of. So soon . . . soon we're gonna have a baby!"

I didn't want to get my hopes up only to be disappointed again . . . but oh, I wanted you. Would the adoption happen?

Of course, it did. And so, weeks later, we were holding you in our arms and thanking God with all our might.

You probably won't be able to understand our joy that day until you hold your own little one in your arms, but believe me—*you did fill* our hearts with joy. And now, eighteen years later, we are *still* rejoicing!

We have never lost the love we felt from the first day on. But even then, we didn't know about all the joy you'd bring into our lives. And when the few hard times came— still, you came through it with flying colors, and so did we! Yesss!

Happy birthday, my dear son. We love you. Your sisters love you—*especially* your sisters. What a wonderful young man you are!

Lovingly,
Mom and Dad

SPECIAL WORDS FOR SPECIAL DAYS

Birthday

Dearest Daughter,

Just as I started to write this birthday note to you, I looked out the window in front of my desk and saw a tiny hummingbird savoring the nectar from some purple blossoms. His feathers were shimmering with brilliant colors, and the nectar must have tasted wonderful, because he hovered almost lazily at each blossom. What a sight!

Is it a coincidence that I saw such a beautiful example of God's creative hand at the exact moment that I was about to write you and tell you how beautiful you are? I don't think so.

Beauty is just one of your gifts, you know. And the great thing is, your beauty shines from your face and out of your eyes from your soul. You are beautiful inside and out!

Now *there's* something to celebrate, and I take double joy in the fact that I can sign this note

Lovingly,
Mom

Birthday

Dearest Debbie,

You know that we've always prayed that our friendship would nurture and nourish us both. And certainly it has!

But today, on your birthday, I pray this mutual friendship of ours will be especially heart warming. You mean so much to me (and my whole family). I wish you a wonderful day and a nourishing year to come.

Your forever friend,

Birthday

My dear Sam,

Okay, I give up! Why don't you just *tell* me what you've learned or seen or felt this past year that has brought change in your life and has made you even *more* of a treasured person?

Tell me, because I want to learn from you.

Happy birthday, dear one.

My love,

Birthday

Our dear Son-in-law,

We wish you joy and a large measure of pure fun on your birthday!

Have a great golf year, ski year, business year, whatever!

We think you're a wonderful person! Keep up the good work!

Our love,

New Year

Dearest Sheri and Paul,

Today, the first day of the new year, I thought of you and wanted you to have my wish list:

I wish for your family's good health.

I wish for the angels of God to protect you all.

I wish for God's blessings on all your endeavors, both at home and at your places of school and work.

But most of all, I wish these words, found in Numbers 6:24–26, to shower your lives with encouragement and hope:

May the Lord bless and protect you; may the
Lord's face radiate with joy because of you;

may he be gracious to you, show you his favor,
and give you his peace.

I wish you a blessed New Year!

Love,

New Year

My dearest Daughter,

I love the way God gives us another chance. Here we
have another year—and oh, yes, I'm well aware of the
joys and sorrows of the last year, but we have been
granted another year of loving and learning, giving and
taking, stretching and growing.

The past *several* years have been very difficult for you,
but I'm so proud and happy for you as you continue your
journey into wholeness. What I want to say for this new
year is this: Listen to the gentle stirrings of your heart, my
dear one. Listen carefully, and don't doubt your intuitions
or the spirit of discernment within you.

I *know* the Lord is with you, and he can be trusted.
Every day I'll hold you up before him, whisper your
name, and trust that his loving, protective care will surround your whole being.

Here's to a blessed new year, darling.

Lovingly, Your mom

Valentine's Day

My dear Cherisher,

Only those who have a cherisher in their lives can know how love and marriage are supposed to be.

You cherishers are few and far between, and I'm thankful that you are mine.

Here's this in writing: I'll *forever* be your cherisher. Valentine's Day or a dreary Monday—no matter. This love of ours is forever and beyond!

Your grateful wife,

❧

Valentine's Day

My dear Husband,

I believe it was the actress Sophia Loren, a very beautiful woman, who said, "Nothing makes a woman more beautiful than the belief that she *is* beautiful."*

Let me tell you, darling, you have used every year of our life together to tell me that you think I'm beautiful.

I think I've got the message—but keep on saying it! I love it!

Happy Valentine's Day, and yes, I'll be your valentine. Your truly-in-love-with-you valentine.

I love you,

---

* *Women & Beauty* (New York: Morrow).

Valentine's Day

Dearest Love,

Everybody knows exactly what I think about you—because when anybody mentions your name, my face shines, reflecting the glow from my heart.

Happy Valentine's Day, darling.

I love you,

Easter

Dearest Jill,

I can hear your beautiful, crystal-clear voice singing a certain song for our Easter services. You know the one—my favorite! Especially the last stanza:

When he comes, our glorious king
All his ransomed home to bring,
Then anew this song we'll sing,
Hallelujah, what a Savior!

All right, now, join together—once more, from the top.

Hallelujah, what a Savior!
Yesss!

Happy Easter, dear Nightingale!

Love,

Easter

My dearest Children and Grandchildren,

I celebrate Easter with you, even though we live several states away from each other.

Nothing can dampen this Easter season.

He is alive! I know so because I talked to him a moment ago. He sends his love and joy to you on this incredibly special day of celebration.

Have a blessed Easter, my dear ones.

Lovingly,
Mom

Mother's Day

Dearest Clare,

Our tendency is to overlook the obvious on Mother's Day . . . we take motherhood for granted, for normal, and for ordinary.

But in our quiet times we can see it takes a woman of courage, of optimism, of great spirit and attitude to bring mothering off.

Mostly though I think mothering like yours happens most often and most beautifully because you are a woman of prayer. And yesterday when I read,

> Thank God for any mother, anywhere
> who loves and serves, and finds her strength in
> prayer,*

I thought of you!

Love,

---

* Grace Noel Crowell, "There Still Are Mothers," *Songs of Faith* (New York/London: Harper & Brothers Publishers, 1939).

Mother's Day

Dear Roseanne,

Happy Mother's Day from one *great* mother to another!

Love,

Mother's Day

Dear Sweet Melissa,

No child support check this month? No reserve for rent, food or kids' clothes? Nothing to set aside for a rainy day?

Help! I suspect your struggles as a single Mom have pushed you into a full blown panic attack. And no wonder!

No financial support. No emotional courage. No shoulder to cry on or arms to hug you. No squelching those self-doubts.

Believe me, I know you and love you and you are one fantastic woman of courage and a *great* mother.

You are always in my prayers to heaven, and on a practical earthly note . . . Yes . . . I'll pick up your kids from school now *and* next fall.

My love,

Mother's Day

Dearest Ruth,

I am well aware of the fact that you and Rollie never had children of your own, but I am also aware that, as a piano teacher and Sunday school teacher, you've had more children than most of us, and you qualify for the Mother's Day Award as few of us can!

Happy Mother's Day to you! You have my gratitude for all the nurturing and loving care you've poured into so many children's lives . . . especially in the case of my own son and daughter!

You are blessed, and so are all the children who know you!

You are loved,

Mother's Day

Dearest Linda,

My heart is with you. I know this is the first Mother's Day without your mom. She was wonderful, and she will always be missed.

Today I've tried to remember all the good times I've had over at your house. Including the day you and I completely trashed the kitchen as we tried to make fudge — what a mess! She tried to act mad at us, remember? But all three of us ended up laughing, scooping and spooning out fudge to each other.

So have a few happy memories today. She was a great mom, and you'll always miss her, but remember . . . you are special, too!

Love,

Mother's Day

Dearest Kim,

Some might say, "What do you know about motherhood? You had a miscarriage . . . you never even *gave* birth."

Please know that your baby qualified you to reflect today on motherhood—even if you didn't have the opportunity to put being a mother to the practical tests of time. You *have* been a mother . . . and so today, as your heart hurts because of the precious little one who left before being born, don't allow anyone to put you down with inappropriate comments.

You were a mother, even if briefly, so I honor you as a mother, and I ask God to hold your baby gently in his arms . . .

My love and prayers,

Mother's Day

Dearest Debbie,

I don't know how you do it. But you do it *so* well!

Being a single mom and carrying that terribly heavy load of responsibility has never been, even for one single second, easily achieved — but you've been an inspiration to me.

I'm proud of you, and I wish you a joyous Mother's Day!

You deserve the best!

Love,

Mother's Day

My darling daughter Laurie,

What always hits me on Mother's Day is how quickly you went from being a little four-year-old scamp (when I asked you for the *third* time to turn off the garden hose, your let's-kiss-and-make-up retort was, "Okay peaches and cream. You are my dream.") to the gifted and courageous mother you are now to James and Jennifer, my delightful grandchildren.

But quick or slow, the reality is you are a *great* mother, and I am pleased, proud, and very grateful you are my daughter.

Happy Mother's Day.

I love you.
Mom XXOO

Mother's Day

Dear Mom,

I know that for years you and I have not seen things eye to eye; we have differed on many issues. It's been painful for both of us, but one thing I think we can agree on as truth is this: You are my mother, and I am your child.

This Mother's Day I am setting aside my biases, my preconceived ideas, and my own conclusions. I want you to know, from my heart, that I honor you as my mother and respect the fact that God put us both together.

Thank you for the time and effort you've put into our relationship. I can and will always care very deeply for you.

Happy Mother's Day.

Mother's Day

My dear Mrs. Holmes,

I know you are not my birth mother, but in many ways, you have been a real mother to me.

You're my real mother because you have always encouraged me to do my *absolute* best. Real, because you believed in my gifts, and your belief was contagious enough to make *me* believe I might be gifted. Real, in that you were like a mother-friend and mentor to me during my teen years when I drove everyone, including myself, crazy.

So to you, dear real and very-special-type Mother, happy Mother's Day!

Love,

Father's Day

Dear Dad,

I looked and looked for the right card for you, and finally found one that's funny and a second one that's serious about our relationship . . .

But I still want to add in my own hand that you really are the best dad in the world—no, make that the universe! I've always thought of you as my protector and defender, and as a caring and sensitive man to Mom, Larry, and me.

Thank you for being truly a man of God for your family!

I'll always be your little girl and your grown-up daughter at the same time. And I'll thank God for every Father's Day we have, so I can say loud and clear: I love you, Dad!

My love,

Father's Day

Dear Dad,

Going Top Ten at the U.S. National Championship accomplished basically all but one professional goal I'd set for myself. I get quite emotional about it even now, because while I was trotting through the gate on that great filly, I could feel your presence right with me. Even as they played the national anthem at the end, I thought of you, and although you didn't know the news yet, I didn't have to wonder how proud you would be — I knew!

Your love and encouragement, always making me feel as though I could do anything I wanted, got me there.

I realize that having good health, enjoying the little things in life, being close to your family, and being right with God are much more important than winning any championship. But winning sure was a lot of fun! The whole time I was in the ring, knowing we were doing well, I thought of you and all the close moments we have shared around horses.

In fact, every time I did well with a horse, and even when I didn't, I always saw that little gleam in your eye as you recognized my dedication and love of horses. It has always been that little gleam that I remember, and the memory keeps urging me to push harder, be smarter, and continue to pursue my dream.

I love you, Dad.

Love,

Graduation

My dear Trevor,

A long time ago I wrote the following words. Today when I ran across them I thought about you standing on the threshold of graduation and wondering what future lies beyond that door. I wrote,

Could the fuzzy
caterpillar know,
Did he ever suspect
or dream,
That one day he would
peel away old lifestyles
and break forth flying into
the future—transformed?

So tell me, dear Trevor, did you ever suspect or dream about the plans God has for you? I have, and believe me, those plans are terrific!

Congratulations on graduating!

Our love,

Graduation

Hello honey,

Just wanted to tell you I don't care what anybody said or what anybody thought!

I knew you could do it! I knew it all along! I'm so proud of you.

Congratulations!

Love,

~

Graduation

My dear wonderful Grandsons,

Since both of you are graduating on the very same night from the very same high school, I'm writing these words so I can *shout* how enormously proud I am of you two.

Actually, I'm proud, pleased, and perfectly silly about the fact that you are *my* grandsons! You are wonderful young men.

I wish your school had asked me to be the commencement speaker for your graduation ceremony. (Relax. They didn't.) That's probably for the best, because most of my speech would be just a brag session about my grandsons. (Well, not really.)

But believe me, if they *did* ask me to speak, I know my

speech would include two important quotes on issues that would realistically assist your emergence into the adult world. Here's what I'd say. (Don't worry. They're short, sweet, and to the point.)

First I would repeat Colin Powell's words about success from *The Black Collegian.* He wrote, "There are no secrets to success. It is the result of preparation, hard work, and learning from failure."

Then I would end the speech with your own great-grandmother's spiritual admonition to "Keep faith with God . . . regardless and always."

So there you have it. A commencement speech from your grandmother, on paper and sent to you both with a world of love and best wishes for your graduation!

You are loved by me,

~

Graduation

My darling April Joy,

In honor of your graduation from high school . . . and because I'm a grandma who loved you before you were born and has every moment since, I put this photo album together for you to enjoy and treasure always.

I went through a mountain of pictures of you and had fun selecting quite a few of my favorites. The album begins with one of the first pictures your dad took of you . . . just a few weeks old . . . in your mom's arms.

Then I put in many of my own treasured photos of you right up to the present time. And, as you'll see, I couldn't resist writing a running commentary alongside the pictures.

Just look at your face . . . your smile and your many expressions of joy! What a beauty you are! As I put the album together, I loved pictorially tracking your beauty from babyhood to now. So here you are, now eighteen years old, a radiant and beautiful young woman inside and out, a 4.0 high school graduate who has just been accepted to Southern California University.

No wonder your parents, your family, and all who know you are so thrilled and proud of you that they are shouting their congratulations to you!

But I think that, next to your mom's and dad's, my grandma's heart swells and beats with pride, love, and absolute joy more than anybody's!

Congratulations, darling girl, and remember . . . *daily* you are in my prayers and in my heart of hearts. I love you.

My love,
Grandma

Wedding

Dearest Debbie and Michael,

This card really says it all, but knowing and loving you and your parents compel me to add this note.

Considering all the young people entering into marriage right now, I believe that because you have faith in God and because you value and treasure the same ideas and goals, your marriage has the most wonderful chance of surviving and thriving until old age finally catches up with you and takes one of you to your heavenly home.

You have our prayers and certainly our best wishes for a long, long life together.

Our love,

Wedding

Dearest Bride and Groom,

I am resisting the temptation to write out an instruction manual for a lasting marriage. It's probably a good decision on my part. You're bound to get an abundance of unsolicited advice from everybody from relatives to the clerk at the grocery store!

What I will say is that when I saw you two at church a few weeks ago, all I could think of was how wonderfully well your spirits seem to mesh. Of course, no couple has a guarantee that their marriage will last and thrive for fifty or more years. But it seems to me that yours has an excellent chance of being one of those rare and lovely marriages between two people who mutually cherish each other . . . and I find that awesome.

My love and prayers go with you.

New Baby

Dearest Michelle,

So her name is Lauren! She sounds wonderful, healthy, and beautiful. What more could we ever ask for in our babies?

Today I read Paul's letter to Timothy about his mother and grandmother. I couldn't help thinking of you and the spiritual inheritance you have to give to Lauren. Remember the passage? It goes like this, with one exception (I changed the names):

> To Michelle,
>   I know how much you trust the Lord, just as your mother, Marion, and your grandmother, Veronica, do; and I feel sure you are still trusting him as much as ever (2 Tim. 1:5).

Both you and Robert will be passing along to Lauren your rich legacy of faith. What a grand opportunity!

You'll be giving Lauren all the right beginnings for her to have a healthy and yes, even holy, life!

You have our love, our prayers, and our heartiest congratulations!

Love,

New Baby

My dear Karen and Mark,

What a wonderful addition to your *already wonderful* family!

Congratulations on Kevin's birth. I know how much you wanted a boy (after four girls), but you wouldn't have blinked an eyelash or skipped a heartbeat if your baby had been a girl. You are great parents—and great parents have normal but great families!

In our church service today they dedicated five babies to the Lord in a short ceremony at the altar. As I looked at those parents, babies, and grandparents, and heard our pastor ask all of us to follow these babies with our love and prayers, I silently vowed yes and said Kevin's name as well.

Congratulations! My, Kevin's in for a really incredible life, isn't he?

Love,

New Baby

My dearest Kim,

My goodness! I just realized I've known you and your family for twenty-some years! You were twelve when we first met. I thought you were beautiful then, and I still do!

I remember attending your birthday and family gatherings, watching you in cap and gown at your high school graduation, seeing you off to Asbury College—in short, watching and loving you through all those years. And you know what . . . you've given me a storehouse of memories.

And while I was disappointed that I was too sick to attend your wedding with Jim (Thank you for the wonderful pictures!), and although I've not seen you in a few years, still, the bonds of love between us have never broken. Nor are they even bent. You all are a regular part of my prayers.

Just today I received your beautiful birth announcement *with pictures* of your first baby—a boy named James Jr.!

Well, all I've got to say is, if he's anything like his parents and his grandparents, James Jr.

will be sterling of heart and character,
will love the Lord and his parents,
and will have your drop-dead good looks.

So naturally, he'll be gorgeous inside and out!

My love and prayers,

P.S. Gift to follow.

~

Get Well

My dear Audrey,

I'm sending you this little porcelain sparrow because I want it to remind you of God's love and mine. You know the song, "His Eye Is on the Sparrow"? Well, it's true—the Lord is watching over you and me!

As you recover from surgery, I thought you might like to read my thoughts on you and your sparrow, so I wrote,

Sometimes
I suffer from occasional
spiritual amnesia, and I forget
the lessons of the sparrows. Sparrows know
who they are. They never try to be eagles.
They know why they are here; they never
tell God how to lead, & from their little bills
down to their tail feathers, they know
exactly whom to trust! They never forget that
it's God who watches over them. Today,
Lord, remind all of us of the sparrows.
For You can be trusted.

So, dear one, during this time of recovery, may you *rest* and *trust* in God's special love for you. Remembering his eye is on the sparrow and knowing he watches over you!

Love,

Get Well

Dearest Joan,

From time to time, as you are in the process of healing recovery, I'm going to send you a little gift, a card, a note, a cartoon, or a Scripture verse that I hope will give you a few moments of relief from the struggle you presently endure.

Today it is this Scripture that rather jumped out of the Psalms at me. It's such a truth, dear Joan, for it says, "O God my Strength! I will sing your praises, for you are my place of safety. My God is changeless in his love for me and he will come and help me" (Ps. 59:9–10).

I love the line about God's changeless love for us! But I love—even more—that he will come and help me . . . yes!

Until you're past this hard place in your recovery, God's with you, and so am I!

My love,

Thanksgiving

My dearest Cherisher,

Here's my gratitude list for this Thanksgiving season. I'm thankful and grateful for:

- The time God has given us to be together.
- The house we call home.
- The intelligence to recognize each other's gifts, talents, and strengths.
- These sensitive hearts of ours that care, not only for each other, but for the hurting people of the world.
- The gift of love that consumes us, which is laced with respect, concern, and nourishment.
- The wonderful children and grandkids God has given us.

Happy, blessed Thanksgiving, dearest one! I'm grateful to God for you.

My never-ending love,

SPECIAL WORDS FOR SPECIAL DAYS

Thanksgiving

Dearest Shar,

What's it been now . . . three Thanksgivings in a row when you come and have dinner with us on *the* day?

We are blessed to have you grace our table with your sparkling self.

None of us know *exactly* how many Thanksgivings or Christmases we will have together, so your being with us gives us an extra reason to be *thankful*!

And believe me, we *are* thankful for you all year round—not just at holiday times.

See you soon. Come hungry!

Love,

~

Christmas

Dearest Susan,

Christmas will be here in a few days. Why is it that when I was a little girl it *never* came soon enough? But oh, my, now that I'm the mama, Christmas (it seems) gets here like *yesterday*! So many things are left undone simply because I've run out of time. Funny thing!

The truth is, the older I get, the more work, fatigue, unpleasant anticipations about family members, and (this is the big one) unrealistic expectations make my stress level zoom to almost unbearable heights.

So this year, I'm writing you this note to tell you I'm going to *try* to remember the *joy* of this celebration, worship the Baby who came that night so long ago, and focus my attention on doing as much as I can without feeling guilty about what I can't do.

And if during *the* big day, I tend to forget my Christmas Plan . . . would you please remind me of this letter?

And perhaps *after* Christmas you and I can just run away together and let someone else clean up the wrapping paper, do the dishes, and take down the Christmas lights, inside *and* out. Okay. So I'm fantasizing . . . but doesn't it sound great? Running away, I mean.

Just kidding. I'll see you Christmas Day. I'll be wearing rings on my fingers and bells on my toes. I can hardly wait to see your beautiful face.

My love,

Christmas

Dearest Leanne,

I could just feel your fears and anxieties coming through your letter.

Anticipating the Christmas family get-together can almost ruin the entire month of December. Particularly if the dinner's at *your* house.

You asked how you can get through Christmas without coming completely unglued and losing what's left of your mind. And you want me to give you some kind of theory, game plan, or strategy for the holiday festivities. Ho, Ho, Ho!

I honestly don't have a wonderful, foolproof plan, only one suggestion. It's worked for me, so perhaps it will work for you . . . at least it might lower your emotional blood pressure and reduce those stress-laden fears.

Right now, today, make a pact with yourself. Promise yourself that you will try to have *realistic expectations* of the people who are coming to your dinner. We get into trouble when we dream or fantasize about everyone loving everyone else, or the dinner being *Better Homes and Gardens*—perfect and amazingly delicious, or Uncle Fred coming clean and sober, or Mother being uncharacteristically sweet to everyone. It probably ain't gonna happen that way!

In other words, *don't* expect your brother Glen [or parent, or other relative] to be charming and agreeable when he's never been that way in the past. He will probably do the same stupid stuff, say the same awful things, and have the same offensive attitude toward others as he's always had.

If you hope, pray, and anticipate that somehow Glen will be different this year, chances are, you'll be terribly disappointed. So don't hope for change. If you're holding no hope for him to change, then when he comes and acts like a jerk, *you'll* be able to say to yourself, "I knew he'd be like that." And you won't find yourself out in the kitchen, alone, heartbroken, and weeping.

Of course, if he comes and—wonder of wonders—he has changed for the better, then Yippee and Hallelujah! It will be the icing on the Christmas cake. At least you won't have hoped in vain—whether he's his old self or Mr. Wonderful. *Not* hoping is about the only way I've ever known to avoid being bitterly frustrated with someone's destructive behavior or words.

I'll get off my soapbox now. But I have seen Glen in action, watched him mutilate your feelings (and those of others) for a long time now. I've faced the fact that we can do nothing to change other people . . . but we can change the pivot point of our own perspectives.

Whoops, I just had another thought. Back to my soapbox for a moment.

Maybe, and I do mean *maybe,* this is the year to give Glen some intangible gifts. Like the gift of respect by accepting his differences and disturbing ways. Hard to do, I know, but if you can accept him as is and try to avoid getting angry with him . . . you might make it through Christmas with less heartache.

Or you could give Glen the gift of empathy. (He probably hasn't received that gift from too many people.) The gift of empathy requires you to stand back then step into his shoes for a moment and see how *he* is feeling. We all long for someone to understand (even a little bit) what life is like for us. Also, I don't know why, but since we feel so *alone* in our despairing circumstances, it's a help to have the empathy of another who has been there, done that.

I'll be thinking of you on Christmas Day, and you can be sure I'll be praying that this Christmas, no matter what Glen does, *you'll* experience the Christ Child's joy and peace during this Christmas season.

You can do it. I just know you can.

My love,

Christmas

Dearest ones,

In view of your beautiful and loving invitation to spend the Christmas holidays with you all, I'm pleased as punch to tell you that Santa isn't the only one who's coming to town. *We* are! Our reindeer will fly in, arriving at the airport (where else?) on Southwest Airlines Flight 180 on Tuesday night, December 23, at 9:35 P.M.

Please bring the Suburban, as we are loaded with gifts! (You should have heard the reindeer moaning about the weight!)

Give the grandkids our advance love, and tell them that our love gauges are wa-a-a-y down and will need lots of hugs and kisses to bring them up and to keep them going for a few months.

Oh, yes, we are looking forward to seeing the Christmas musical at your church—and we can hardly wait to see you all!

Our love,

Special Words of Thanks

~

My dear Reader,

Somehow I think thank-you notes rank at the top of the list as being the most perfunctory, boring, and impersonal notes of all time.

Take my own eight-year-old effort, written at my mother's patient insistence . . .

Dear Aunt Harriett,

Thank you for the $1 you gave me for my birthday.

Love,

Joyce

The next year, when I accidentally skipped the thank-you note, my mother got an indignant call from a disgruntled Harriett, so the following year, when I was a bit wiser and a dollar richer, I wrote my note and was proud of myself for adding three more words.

Dear Aunt Harriett,
    Thank you for the $1 you gave me for my birthday. I like it.

                                  Love,
                                  Joyce

So much for perfunctory, boring, and impersonal . . . we all know how to write *those* thank-you's!

Over the years the notes of thanks that have meant the most to me seemed to have three ingredients in common. They had a way of saying "thank you" that was at once warm and comforting, yet sincere:

1. They usually begin with "you" or "your" sentences. An opening like that tends to get one's attention up front—right away.
2. They name the gift, favor, or thoughtful act. They are specific (which is wonderfully helpful because by the time a thank-you note arrives, most of us have forgotten what we gave or did).
3. They end by writing out the words *thank you.* And I suspect if they weren't too crazy about the gift I'd given them, they covered it nicely by thanking me for "caring" or for "investing time and money" and so on. In short, they acknowledged my gift-giving *effort,* no matter what it had been.

When you think about it, saying "thank you" and expressing our gratitude is, in itself, a tender gift. It's especially so when started early in our homes with our families. But more than that, saying or writing our thank-you's can be a tiny, quiet interlude amid the frantic hustle and bustle of our daily lives.

In fact, "thank you" well may be just exactly the kind and thoughtful words of encouragement one needed to hear—at precisely the right moment. And not in the least bit perfunctory, boring, or impersonal!

Love,

Joyce

~

For Christmas Gift

My darling Grandma,

On Christmas Day, when you pressed the two one-dollar bills into my hand, you apologized (in Hungarian yet) that it wasn't more. But, dear Grandma, I know you are on a fixed income! Besides, there is no need to give me a gift of money anyway!

Just our being together is a fine and wonderful thing. I thank God for every Christmas you have here on this earth.

Thank you for the money gift, but I'd just rather have you around for a few more years! I love you . . . always!

Love,

For Christmas Gift

Dearest Marilyn-honey,

You're the greatest sister a woman could ever have! Besides, your gifts, which reflect your attention to details, are always a joy to unwrap!

The beautiful candlestick, in its gorgeous white holder decorated with silk flowers, is on our dining room table now. The chocolate-covered cherries, however, are gone: they were eaten within seconds of being unwrapped. Oh, yes, I thought the pin and earrings set was, like you, beautiful.

Thank you for your lovely gifts, but more, thank you for your love! You're the best!

Lovingly,
Your sister

For Christmas Gift

Dearest Aunt Celeste,

How is it you *always* know exactly what I like? I'm really into angels this year, so your angel calendar was just perfect.

It's on my desk, and I have to smile because, even though you live a long way away, it brings you to mind instantly. It's not as good as really seeing you, but close.

Thank you! I love being your niece.

My love,

For Birthday Gift

Dearest Roseanne,

No one, I repeat, no one has ever before invited me and four other February birthday women to celebrate in a beautiful tea room for the English version of high tea.

But *you* did! And we were delighted with the sandwiches (I especially loved the cucumber and cream cheese), the fragrant and delicious selection of teas (ginger peach, my favorite), and the array of totally obscene desserts (I inhaled the chocolate and fresh strawberry number).

Thank you! You made us all feel fortunate to be alive and gave us more than a tea cup of loving encouragement to go for another year!

I adore being your friend,

For a Birthday Gift

My dear Lois,

You paid for lunch! I know it was my birthday, but you took it upon yourself to pick up the check. What a woman! And what a friend!

Your birthday and Paulette's are coming up in the next few months, and *I* intend to pay for the honored privilege. Don't even *think* about it in any other way!

Thank you! I had a *wonderful* time and your company, lunch, and your gifts took the sting out of having yet *another* birthday. By George, I think I'll make it for another year!

My love,

~

For a Birthday Gift

My dearest Husband,

I know what I said: "Honey, for my fortieth birthday don't do anything special. I'll be very happy with the newly painted walls and beautiful border paper in our family den and laundry room . . ." But I lied.

Forty scares me a bit, and as I thought about it, I realized what I'd really like is something special to mark the event and to help ease the pain!

But bless your sweet heart, you guessed my heart's

desires, and you took my mom with you to the store and bought the ring I'd oohed and ahed over last week.

Then you completely surprised me at my birthday dinner by having the waitress slip the ring over the candle on my piece of cake. I was stunned and clearly surprised. (I'd talked myself into the "den and laundry room" present.)

Of course I love the ring, but please know I love you even more! Especially since you didn't pay any attention to what I said about the den.

Your spirit and heart full of love toward me and our kids are just awesome.

I love you,

〜

For a Birthday Gift

My darling Wife,

I said it, and I'll say it again and again: You are *the* most incredible human being in the history of the universe. "That's an overstatement," you say? I don't think so.

You went to a great deal of time, effort, and labors of love to make my birthday unique. And while I said, "Please don't fuss for my birthday," you managed to surprise and delight me with a great celebration!

I'm blessed to have you as my wife. Thank you, darling, for the gifts (I love the shirt), the candlelight dinner, and the special joy of just being together!

I love you,

For a Birthday Gift

My dear son Rick,

The photo album you made for me with the running story and pictures of you as a child is a treasured gift I'll never throw away or stop appreciating!

Where did you find all those pictures, and who taught you to write such great copy? I loved the humorous touches you added to the pictures with your funny, funny comments.

It's a birthday card to end all birthday cards, but mostly I love that my son thought it all out and then sent his original work to me. Thank you, Rick-honey.

I really like and love being your mom!

My love always,

For a Birthday Gift

My darling Laurie,

I'm not sure how you do it, only that my mother did it with me.

You unfailingly know what gifts will please the day-lights out of me! How do you do that?

I can count on the fact that whatever you decide to get me for my birthday will be "just perfect," "exactly what I wanted," or that "it looks like you, Mom" and it screamed, "Buy me, buy me!" as you walked by.

You just can't help yourself, can you? You keep adding to my memory's frozen-picture gallery.

You are the world's most delightful daughter and—surprise of all surprises—God chose me to be your mother!

Lovingly,

Your mom

For Wedding Gifts

Dear Mr. and Mrs. Claremont,

What a wonderful wedding gift your [vase, toaster, etc.] was. Not only that, but it was thoughtful of you to take the time, the energy, and the money to send it with your warm wishes for our marriage. We are grateful.

Thank you for contributing to our wedding-day joy.

Love,

On Mother's Day

My dearest Daughter,

Your Mother's Day phone call [or letter or visit] reminded me of a time when you and your brother were teenagers.

Remember the day Grandpa came to our house and announced he couldn't attend your brother's wedding (three months away) because, as a pastor, he'd scheduled a church picnic for that day?

You undoubtedly *do* remember. Especially the long, drawn-out argument and the harsh words. But after he left, what happened next is a wonderful memory for me, your mom. I fled into the living room, sank down on the couch, and sobbed my heart out. Not a heartbeat later, you came and put your arms around me, reversing the mother-daughter roles. Without a word, you sat down and wept with me.

Today your phone call did the same thing—comforted my heart, made me feel valued as a person and honored as a mother, and soothed the present ache in my heart with the healing balm of love.

I love you, darling daughter.

Lovingly,
Mom

To My Stepmother

My dearest Elizabeth,

For twenty-two years you took such good care of Daddy. You stood by his side, both physically and emotionally. My brother, sister, and I will always be grateful for the loving heart-care you poured into your marriage with Dad.

You truly loved each other, and when we look back and remember your years with him, we all are filled with admiration, respect, and grateful hearts. Thank you, dear Elizabeth.

You are dearly loved and treasured,

~

To My Stepmother

Dear Ida Rose,

I *know* this is a typical Mother's Day card, but there were no "Stepmother" cards. However, I think this card is perfect because it says it so well: "Happy Mother's Day, from your *Daughter*."

I love you, dear Ida Rose. You are with me every day.

We are all cheering for you regarding cancer [or some other serious illness]. You know we all realize this can happen to any one of us.

I'm so proud of your courage! I hope some of yours will rub off on me. Take care of yourself!

Love,

To My Stepdaughter

Darling Girl,

No matter how old you are, divorce is a shattering process—maybe even more so for the children than the parents. Being a stepdaughter or stepparent is often just as scary, carrying its own kind of brokenness. Which brings me to you.

I know for a fact that it was not easy to accept me as your father's wife—much less your stepmother—but somehow you did it! Somehow you found the courage to give me a chance.

You sensed that in no way did I want to usurp your mother's place—I just wanted to be accepted for who I was, to build our own relationship. I'm not sure how, at such a tender age, you figured that all out—I just know that you did.

Walt Disney's picture of a wicked stepmother in *Cinderella*, based on the Grimm's fairy-tale concept, has never been mine. I thank God that it wasn't yours, either.

Thank you for giving me the chance to know you and for the beautiful, generous, and special gift of love you've given to me!

My love, your not-so-wicked stepmother,

On Father's Day

Dear Son,

Your Father's Day card and letter came on a day when I was feeling quite . . . well . . . not worthless, but without much value.

Your words changed all that in an instant!

Thank you. What a great son you are!

Love,
Dad

~

On Father's Day

Dear wonderful Old Man,

Now that I'm married with two wonderful kids, I'm just *beginning* to understand what a great job you did fathering my sisters and me.

It's scary sometimes—the responsibility of fatherhood, I mean—but I have only to look back at your examples, and I feel certain I'll make it! Happy Father's Day!

I love you, Dad . . . and thanks for showing me the way!

Love,
Your son

SPECIAL WORDS OF THANKS

From a Father

My dear Son,

My college diploma has been packed away for many years, but the letter from you, far more precious than any diploma, is framed and hanging on my office wall.

It's in plain view because, when I see it, I'm reminded of who you are as a person, how you relate to others, and what kind of a man you've become. And I'm grateful to God for giving you to me!

I'm proud and honored to be your dad, and believe me, no college diploma could ever bring such pleasure.

Love,
Dad

To My Stepfather

My dear Earl,

Great stepfathers like you, who do such a loving and caring job, are rarely given the credit they deserve. Like Rodney Dangerfield—they don't get no respect.

I want to change that trend right now. Right here.

You are a wonderful stepdad to me, but I love you and thank you from the depths of my soul for taking such good care of my mom.

In my heart of hearts I know and believe that when she dies she will have ended with the very best—you!

And I will always be grateful.

Love,

❧

To a Prospective Employer

Dear Mr. Howard,

I'm aware that you are interviewing a number of people for the secretarial position at your company, and as you know, I'm taking my resume to others as well—but I wanted to write out this note to you to express my appreciation.

I thoroughly enjoyed the opportunity to meet and talk with you, and if you find me an acceptable candidate, I would be honored to work for you and your company. Thank you for taking the time to consider my qualifications.

Sincerely,

To an Employer

Dear Mr. Stuart,

I know you have my formal letter of resignation, but I wanted to write a personal note for your eyes only. Just because this is how I truly feel.

While I was employed at your company I enjoyed a number of things—friendships with Lois, Al, and John Mark; the staff meetings and conferences; and the many professional and personal lessons I was privileged to learn. I'm grateful even for the painful ones. But all in all I thank you, my boss, for the experience of working for you and your company.

I know I'll draw on these memories many times in the years ahead, so please know you've added a valuable dimension to my life. Thank you!

Warmly,

To an Employer

Dear Mr. Mitchell,

I realize you gave us all a bonus this year—you're a great boss! Your great gift (above and beyond my weekly pay check) is going to enable me to pay for some things I would really like, such as reupholstering our couch—

without feeling guilty that I'm spending and depleting family funds.

Thank you for the bonus, but also, thank you for the generous spirit that surrounded the check itself. I have learned much from you this past year, and I thank you for that also!

Bless you,

❧

To a Former Employee

My dear Merikay,

While you didn't work for us for very long (you moved to another state—how *could* you?), I can still clearly recall how your spirited sense of humor, your wonderful positive attitude, and your humble willingness to tackle any and every task affected our company.

I loved the staff meetings where an issue, a concern, or a new procedure was voiced, and you—with your great attitude—cheerfully emerged. You said things like:

"Okay. I see the problem. . . . I'll get right on it. If *I* can't solve it, then I'll find out who can."

And when you thought you made mistakes at various points along the way, you were quick to apologize and take responsibility. Whatta woman!

Thank you for your large contribution to us here in the workplace and personally to me, here in my heart.

You are missed.

Love,

After the Funeral

Dear Pastor [Monsignor, Father, Rabbi] Smith,

Your remarks [prayers] at my mother's funeral were warm, comforting, and very like you. I have a tape of the service, so in the weeks and months ahead, I will be able to replay your grief-healing words again and again.

Right now I'm still unable to fully realize that she's gone, but your message will carry me a long way toward the process of moving on with my life.

Thank you. Your message was *more* than mere words. It touched my heart.

Warmly,

~

After the Funeral

Dear Norma and George,

You *knew* that flowers would touch my heart, didn't you? They were so fresh and fragrant, and I loved reading the card you sent with them. During the funeral, when I could stand no more the heaviness of grief, I searched out your bouquet and, for a few seconds, saw only its beauty. What sweet relief it brought me in that moment.

Thank you. Your flowers said that you are with me and that you care. I loved that.

Love,

After the Funeral

Dear Eleanor and Ruth,

I've lost track of all the delicious dinners, cakes, and casseroles you brought to my house while I was pregnant with David and after his death, but I'll never lose track of how precious you two are.

Thank you. Your hearts always find unique ways to heal mine.

My love,

After the Funeral

Dearest Betty,

After the funeral, when most of the mourners had gone home or back to their jobs and busy lives, you left your responsibilities, came to my door, and asked, "What do you want me to do today—the dishes or the laundry?"

Thank you. Your love is so practical, it's exquisite!

My thanks! And my love!

57

SPECIAL WORDS OF THANKS

After the Funeral

Dearest friend Perky,

One year after David's death, even though he lived only one day, you knew the mother's heart in me would still be breaking. So you set a huge azalea plant, bursting with hot-pink blossoms, on my porch.

Your card read "In remembrance of David," and oh, how good it felt that someone else understood the lonely place in my heart and filled it with such a beautiful gift!

Thank you. I'll never forget you or your healing gesture.

Love,

To My Pastor

Dear Pastor Jim,

It isn't possible for you to know how your note [or visit or phone call] touched me. What timing!

I feel as if I'm trapped in a revolving nightmare, one from which I may *never* awake. What I struggle with most is the *ongoingness* of it all—one wave, one blow, one storm of agony after another. Will it *ever* end?

Yet, what can anyone but God do? Nothing, really. I think the reason your note means so much to me is that (1) you cared enough to push past my self-protective

SPECIAL WORDS

walls and reach out to me, and (2) your message, loud and clear, is that I must not give up, but continue onward.

Thank you for listening to the still, small voice of the Lord within you telling you to write me. I will always remember and treasure your note!

My love and thanks,

To My Pastor's Wife

Dearest Lois,

Is it a bit lonely living in that pastoral fishbowl? I would suspect it is.

How you dress and do your hair.

How you raise [or discipline] your children.

How you relate to your husband, who not only has feet of clay, but often tracks mud in on your freshly washed kitchen floor.

How you do, or do not, teach Sunday school.

How many services or church events you do or do not attend.

How talented or gifted you are or are not.

How you handle wearing several hats, at home and at church.

You're constantly being scrutinized and evaluated by someone. But what I notice is how great you are to everyone. Believe me, *how* you still have a genuine (and gorgeous) smile and comforting word—for your family and others, including me—is just awesome!

Thank you for being God's woman. You are in my prayers. I send, with this note, a big thank-you in honor of your beauty and your brains. Thanks, too, for being such a great role model for all of us.

Love,

To My Doctor

Dear Dr. Harrison,

You deserve a million pats on the back and a verbal stream of "'Atta boy!"s for the way you listen and take my illness seriously, even the smallest of my complaints. Thank you!

It occurs to me that if you consistently do this for me, you're probably doing it for others as well. So I think you may need to hear that you *are* doing a good job, you *are* meeting and dealing with your patients' needs, and (best of all) you *are* a healing physician—not just a doctor!

Thank you for making a difference in my life as I struggle with this pain. And oh, yes, your nurses and your office staff have caught your caring heart-spirit—they are wonderful, too.

'Atta boy, Doc!

Warmly,

To a Medical Staff Person

My Dear Angie:

Virtually every time you were on duty during the past six months of my chemotherapy, you successfully put that IV needle into my tiny, collapsible veins on your very first try. No easy feat, but you did it with professional grace and skill like no one else could!

I know this for a fact because, on days I went in for treatment and you *weren't* there (oh no!), it seldom failed: someone else would eventually get the needle in, but only after two, three, or four painful, bruising sticks.

So, my hat's off to you, dear One-Stick Angie! Thank you for the compassion you've showered on me! I really needed you, and I'll always be grateful.

You are loved,

To My Dentist

My dear dedicated dentist,

Yes, I know everybody has some form of fear, or even a phobia, about going to the dentist. It's especially true for those of us who've had some pretty awful experiences—but that's not the case with my dental visits to you and your wonderful staff.

You all seem to understand our fears and biases against

dentistry, as much as we might desperately need your help. You go to great lengths to be understanding and tolerant. You're good at explaining procedures (even if we don't get all the technical details), and—maybe best of all—none of you minimize our anxiety or act as if we are just spoiled kids making up our pain or discomfort.

Thank you for the patience you practice with your patients. Thank you, too, for your extraordinary dentistry skills, and for the high priority you and your staff place on professional excellence!

Keep up the great work . . . we need you!

Warmly,

To an Acquaintance

Dear Howard,

Your articles on the newest of alternative methods for cancer patients came yesterday.

Thank you for taking the time to collect and send me this information. Thank you, too, for understanding that I need all the literature, suggestions, medical road maps, and help I can get.

My doctors tell me *I* am the one who must make the choices here for my life . . . but I can only do that with tons of information. Thank you for your sensitive input!

Bless you!

Thanks,

To an Acquaintance

Dear Joan,

I can hear the sentiment of your heart because I read your letter carefully, several times.

You are upset (or at least concerned) because you feel I'm not trusting the Lord enough in my present dire circumstances. You make a good point, but I need to tell you my personal take on the issues.

With me the problem is not a matter of my trusting God. I do trust him. It's just that when one descends into the dark pit of grief or fear it's really hard to tell if and what rescue operation is going on in the clear air and light above you.

So I'm writing this note to assure you that I do love and trust God. I know that no circumstance of yours or mine is beyond God's miraculous reach. And mostly I want to verify that what I really want—and yes, need—are your prayers on my behalf.

Thank you for caring enough to comfort me and to voice your concerns. I thank you also for your petitions to our heavenly Father during these dark days.

In his love,

To My Neighbors

My dear Nelsons,

I know I could run over and bring you a pie, a plant, or some gift, but this is one time when I think written words are best.

You've been *wonderful* neighbors! I run out of fingers and toes counting up all the times you've made that word *neighbor* come to life in the truest sense!

You were neighbors in ways little and big—making a stream of encouraging phone calls over the years, looking after my children from time to time, Bob offering to drive Laurie and me to the emergency room after she stood (I can't believe it!) on a glass and almost cut her heel off, and yes, surreptitiously placing plants at my front door in times of grief or dropping off a beautifully decorated cake to brighten up a special occasion. All your actions were so special.

I thank you for those warm and wonderful memories of bygone days when we were neighbors.

I'll never forget you all.

Love,

To My Friend

Dear Caroline,

Have you noticed that certain words from special people can change your mental (sometimes even your physical) well-being?

You did that today for me. Turned my attitude from surly to sunny! I'm truly grateful! Thank you, dear one.

Love,

To My Friend

Dearest Barbara,

It's funny, even strange, but true.

I can be feeling totally depressed, depleted of all energy, and then you phone.

I hear your voice, listen to your words, and suddenly I'm energized. I'm ready to fight the day's battles. You've stripped away some of my self-doubt. You've infused me with doses of hope that leave me eager to be the person God intended me to be.

Talk about a "new lease on life"! Somehow you are able to make that *lease* a lovely gift to me in each conversation we have.

How do you do that?

My love,

To My Friends

Dear ones,

Although I thanked you by phone the other day for your generous (and unexpected) gift, I wanted to write it out on paper so you could see it in black and white. How did you know that we were in desperate straits and had no idea how we could meet our bills? Your gift came as if it were sent from God in direct answer to our prayers!

Your generosity is topped only by your love and insightful understanding. Sarah and I have thanked God over and over for allowing our paths to cross and mingle, because we have seen so much of the Lord in you two!

Thank you again for your expression of love! Looking forward to seeing you next Friday.

Our love and gratitude,

Special Words
to the Grieving

~

My dear Reader,

It's no wonder that most of us are a little gun-shy about communicating with one who is grieving.

Sadly enough, there have been times in all our lives when we sincerely tried to comfort someone about his/her losses and seriously missed the mark. And sometimes as well-meaning as we are, we simply haven't a clue as to how painful or inappropriate our comments are, nor are we aware of the silent response in the heart of one who is grieving.

Here are some well-meant comments from some well-meaning people who attempted to comfort me when I was grieving:

"Well, how are you doing? Are you over it yet?" (No. I'm not *over* it and today I feel I'll *never* be over it.)

"Your mother is in heaven, so she's better off, and you'll see her again someday!" (But she isn't *here*. I can't pick up the phone and hear her voice.)

"At least your baby isn't suffering anymore." (True, but why did David have to suffer in the first place? Your words are of very small comfort.)

"Are you feeling any better now that it's been six months since the funeral?" (No, grief is not a temporary illness like the common cold, which generally goes away after seven days!)

"When are you going to get back to normal and come to choir practice again?" (What is normal? I have to establish a brand-new "normal" for myself, and who knows? I may *never* come back to choir!)

"Well, at least your baby son won't grow up, become a teenager, and get into trouble, drugs, and violence." (*Trouble, drugs, and violence?* Who knows what he would have become, given a chance? And what makes you so sure that my son would grow up to be a juvenile delinquent, anyway?)

"God needed another rose for his heavenly garden, so he picked yours." (Rubbish! The God I serve is not that cruel or mean spirited, and besides, if he "needed" a flower, he would have said the word and created one on the spot out of thin air!)

"You don't need to be so down in the dumps! After all, you'll see your loved one again in heaven." (Forgive me if I don't tap dance on the table over your words. And please, don't tell me how I should feel right now until a dear and treasured loved one of *yours* is in heaven, leaving you behind here on earth.)

Okay, I'll get off my paper soapbox now, because you get the point, I'm sure. But make no mistake about it — comforting others is a delicate and fragile assignment.

I hope the suggestions that follow and this book's notes to the grieving will be of some help to you.

- Keep your notes and actions simple.
- Keep in mind that we *are* comforted by the love and genuineness of these few words: "I'm sorry about your loss."
- Always write out the name of the deceased. It's comforting to know others still *remember* Bob's or Susan's name.
- Recall some incident you experienced with the deceased. Something funny, thoughtful, or profound. Reminisce about a moment or a day. Recount a memory, or tell how you first met the deceased.
- Don't worry about your notes making grievers cry.

SPECIAL WORDS TO THE GRIEVING

It's too late to avoid that. They are already crying. Let them. Tears often bring about a much-needed emotional release by rinsing out some of the stress and tension *during* the grief process.

Now a few words of caution. Try to stay away from old and tired phrases, clichés, advice, solutions, and out-of-context, overworked spiritual platitudes. I'm not saying these things are never to be used, but use them sparingly to make a stronger message of comfort. Those in grief have probably heard it all before anyway.

And last, but perhaps most important, we must not minimize another's losses or fears, and we dare not judge another's state of mind and heart.

Writing a note to the grieving is throwing a life preserver called comfort and sanity to a person who feels as if he or she is all alone, drowning, and going down for the third time.

Is there anything more honorable or right than throwing out a life preserver to a grieving soul and bringing him or her back to the safety of the shore?

I doubt it.

Love,

Joyce

Loss of Mother

My dear friend Paulette,

A lady at church [job, school, etc.] told me that you seem to be doing very well since your mother's death. She added, "Paulette's really got it all together!"

I thought, "How nice. But is that really true, or is she like most of us—trying to paint a bright, pink, happy face over a sad, dark, purple heart?"

No matter how well you're doing, I believe no one, not even Billy Graham or the pope, has it "all together" all the time.

So, until you are stronger and more able to be "up," even in the darkest part of the night, please know I'm with you and wait with you until we both see the sun come up once more.

You are loved,

Loss of Mother

Dearest Ruth,

Mother's Day this month must have been terribly diffi-cult for you. I knew your mom and understood so well your great relationship with her.

Both your mother and mine were keepers (as they say about great loved ones), so this May when others have their mothers, it's only right that we grieve for our losses and miss our mothers terribly.

Your mother (like mine) has left you with a vast inheritance. Of course, I don't mean money and valuables. I mean you have the lilting sound of her laugh and her sense of humor. You have her kind yet honest way of speaking from the heart, and certainly you've got her hang-in-there spirit! You've even been left (maybe it's in the genes) her gift of expressing strong positive attitudes, which she softened by an amazing amount of graciousness.

The best thing to do with your inheritance is to enjoy it—then give it away. So I encourage you to pull out all the stops, enjoy your special heritage, and then when you're ready, discover the joy and satisfaction of passing on those gifts to loved ones.

You will always miss your mother, but being her daughter and knowing her have made you rich beyond words. We have both been blessed with our mothers and their extraordinary love!

My love,

Loss of Father

My dear Lois,

I know your dad [or other relative] was your Irregular Person. I would have wished for you that somehow before he died, years of unfinished business, old wounds, and haunting and disturbing questions could have been discussed, perhaps resolved. But that was not to be, and now he's gone.

You are bound to feel that this resolution will never happen now, but maybe it can. Because I know you so well, I feel comfortable making a suggestion: You could have your own private memorial service. It could be a time for your heart to heal and find closure. You might try this, but remember, this is just a suggestion.

In a quiet place deep in your heart, acknowledge:

> That he was who he was—your father.
> That you wish things had been far different.
> That you can remember and be grateful for
>   something (even if it's just one little thing) he
>   said or did.
> And finally, that you are telling him good-bye
>   and that now you are releasing him into
>   God's care.

Then lay something of beauty—like a flower or a special piece of music—on his grave or just imagine it in your mind. This offering may give you closure and leave your own heart in a state of peace.

Who knows? These simple rituals may make the phrase "May he rest in peace" come true for both of you.

My love,

Loss of Husband

My dear Sarah,

Even though I have lost loved ones, I can't begin to imagine the black cloud of loneliness hovering over your heart right now. John's death is going to take a long time to sink into my mind. It will take even longer, I know, to sink into yours. His death was so sudden, so completely unexpected.

I will miss him always, but you will miss him even more. . . . You have my heart.

My love,

~

Loss of Husband

Dear Diana,

It's been one [week, month, or year] since you lost your cherisher, Paul. I don't pretend to understand the loss you must be feeling.

I will always remember [his smile, his way of telling stories, an incident that's real and precious], and I find myself wishing he was still here. Of course, I'm grateful that he's not suffering anymore and grateful that I knew him, but I wish I could help fill the vacant place in your heart. I know I can't, but I wish . . . oh, how I wish.

My love,

Loss of Husband

My dear Judy,

Seeing and talking to Bob a few days before he died was an experience I'll always cherish.

When I was at your home for a visit, you told me that he had asked you to move him out of the bedroom and into the family room. So you did. You helped him out of bed and eased him into his favorite recliner chair. I'll never forget the picture. You, standing behind his chair, smoothing his hair once in a while, your knowing glances telling all of us time was swiftly running out.

What I won't forget, either, is the presence of hovering angels we felt as we talked. I told Bob I loved him and had wonderful memories of his work at our church and on my board. I reminded him about the time, years ago, that he asked me to speak at his singles Sunday school class in our church. And even though he was so sick, remember, Judy, he chuckled a bit and slowly remarked that it was so strange that until he asked, no one had asked me to speak. "And that," he shook his head slightly, "was when you were speaking *all over the world,* but no one had ever asked you to speak at your own home church!" I had loved him then for asking me to speak, and I loved him then for the memory of his remembering the irony of the event.

Everyone tells me, dear Judy, that you're doing remarkably well. I knew you would. You have always had class and dignity. But on the days when holding your

SPECIAL WORDS TO THE GRIEVING

head up high and "moving on" (as they say) with your life is just too ridiculously painful, I believe it's perfectly all right to sit down in the middle of the road and grieve. I'll join you anytime you want, and together we can recall Bob's beautiful spirit the day he wanted to be out in the family room.

My love to you and until we see him again, you are in my prayers,

Loss of Wife

My dear Sam,

I still can't believe my long-time, treasured friend Betsy is gone. Forgive me if it takes me a while to accept it.

As her husband, you had a lot more time with her than I did. And, of course, so did your children and grandkids. But the time I did have with her—through almost thirty years of phone calls, letters, and all-too-brief visits—are priceless, frozen pictures in my mind.

I'm trying to take out and thaw those pictures of Betsy today. I want to see them clearly, to remember those delicious and happy times with her. But it's hard. Maybe when my eyes quit stinging from the unstoppable flow of tears, maybe then I'll be able to look at those images, smile, and enjoy her all over again.

We both know we'll see Betsy in heaven, but what I don't know is if I can wait that long!

I'm holding you up in my prayers, dear Sam, now more than ever.

Love,

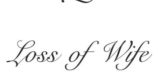

Loss of Wife

Dear John,

By real and painful experience I know that time does *not* heal all wounds, as so many people are quick to assert.

So, I'm hoping that my love for you may heal at least some parts of your breaking heart as the days and nights drag by. You're in my prayers . . . always.

Love,

Loss of Son

My dear Linda,

The diagnosis of cancer or Alzheimer's strikes a universal fear in all our hearts . . . but AIDS? That name is positively terrifying. And what's worse, as you are finding out since David's death, is the ugly stigma that not only has attached itself leechlike to your precious son's memory but is siphoning out the very lifeblood from your heart!

SPECIAL WORDS TO THE GRIEVING

Why is it that we have to burn the word *AIDS* like a cattle brand across people's foreheads? When will we realize that it is not our job to judge, to place blame, or to pull our skirts righteously around us and snidely pronounce, "Well, no one in *my* family would ever be HIV-positive, much less get AIDS!" When will we put into practice the so-called "forgiving attitude" we claim to have as people of God? When will we accept and love AIDS sufferers and their families *as they are*?

That was the gist of what a friend of mine said today. She, who works with parents of homosexuals and has watched as AIDS has wiped away the lives of so many, said, "All you can do is love them *as they are!*" And I thought, *That's probably the true meaning of John 3:16: For God so loved the world* . . .

You won't find any rejection, incrimination, blame, or judgment pronounced here . . . only a spirit of grace, of love, and of prayers for you and your shattered dreams.

I'm with you. And one more thing: David was a wonderful human being! And so are you!

My love,

Loss of Daughter

Dearest Connie,

This is your first Christmas [or Hanukkah] without your darling daughter Janet. Of course, you miss her all the time, but somehow this season seems to intensify the pain of grief.

Now, while you anticipate trying to sing carols, wrap and give presents, go to a Christmas Eve service, or decorate the tree and house, your heart must be devastated by the shroud of grief because . . . well, because Janet won't be there with you. Maybe you feel that if you allow any of the joy of Christmas to show on your face or in your actions, somehow you are being disloyal to Janet, especially since she can no longer enjoy and share this special time with you.

However, in my heart I have a quiet assurance that our loved ones . . . your Janet . . . are with us in spirit. And I feel it comforts them to see us carrying on with the beautiful traditions of Christmas.

Even though my mother died many years ago, I occasionally feel her presence. Like last Christmas as I finished decorating a small tree for our table. I recall stepping back and being pleased with something . . . and then I realized I could feel my mother's approval and praise over my decorating skills. And *I* was comforted. I pray this for you with Janet.

I know that occasionally at Christmas, right in the middle of the festivities, I've felt a little guilty because there was laughter and joy in my house and yet my loved one was gone. By the end of Christmas Day, I suspect your own heart will have grown terribly weary with trying to keep the spirit of Christmas alive for the children and grandchildren. At the same time, you'll be trying to ward off the loneliness engulfing you because of your constant awareness of Janet's vacant chair or the absence of the lovely sound of her voice.

What I really want you to know is that when Christmas Day does come, I'll have a small ceremony in my heart to remember Janet. And for you, dear Connie, I'll light a small candle and ask God to carry you gently through Christmas as painlessly as possible. Then I'll try to visualize how Janet must be celebrating Christmas in heaven. (It's got to be incredibly better than our celebrations here!)

Next Christmas, I'll remember Janet and you in the same way and with the same request of God.

Today, I send my love,

Loss of Child

Dearest Becky,

Somehow it never feels right when your child dies ahead of you. A child *before* a mother? I don't think so. It's not supposed to happen in that sequence. The rule is that grandparents go first, parents next, and then, finally, the children and grandchildren.

The loss of Megan, only nine years old, makes no sense at all.

Yes, we can take some comfort in the memory that her star shone brightly while she was here. And we can recall how God moved through the bone cancer and the chemo and all the times he touched lives *because* of Megan's illness. But that knowledge gave all of us only a temporary reprieve from the raging ache inside, and now, it gives you only a blink of light in the black pit of loneliness that you must be continually falling into.

I'm not going to say, "If there's anything I can do, just call me." (I know you won't call.) But I am going to tell you that it is all right to lean on others when the grieving path is too steep to climb. Here, take my hand and my heart . . . we'll take this journey together.

You have my love and prayers,

Loss of Grandchild

Dearest Marilyn,

The grandma's heart in you must feel like it's beating sluggishly in some kind of dark and heavy coma.

To believe that your grandson Bryan is gone . . . just as he was about to (eagerly!) start his first day at kindergarten can't possibly be true. It's an appalling, macabre joke. Right? No.

How could this freak accident [or harrowing disease] have taken him so quickly [or lingered so long]? I wish I could give you some feel-good answers, or better yet, I wish I could wave a magic wand or turn back the hands of a clock and make this all disappear. But, sadly, I don't have the ability to do either . . . nor does anyone else.

The awful reality is that Bryan isn't here with you as you once knew him to be. After your heart has had a chance to work and push through some of the shocking outrage of it all, please know I'll be praying that little "moments of memories" will strengthen you as you try to deal with his death.

I hope you'll see Bryan in your mind's eye as he was on the day you helped out Karen by picking him up from preschool. Remember how his little face absolutely lit up with joy when he caught sight of you?

"Grandma!" he yelled, and then to Miss Judson he explained, "My grandma's here!" He ran toward you . . . arms flung wide open.

One day, when you're going through heaven's gates, don't be surprised to see Bryan's face light up and to hear him call out, "Grandma, Grandma!" And then to everyone else, with pride in his voice, "My grandma's here!"

What a reunion you two will have!

My love until that day,

After a Miscarriage

My dear Debbie,

You didn't even see her [or his] face, hug her close, or watch her fall asleep in your arms. That's the unbearable way it is with miscarriages. But make no mistake about it, you are a mother, and that baby was your child.

I don't want to be one of those people who pats you on the back and admonishes you not to worry, "You're young; you can have other babies." Nor am I going to say, "Well, at least you have other children." Words like those can come across as insensitive at best, unnecessarily cruel at worst.

So what I am going to say to you, dear one, is simply this: You have lost a baby, and you will probably always feel that loss. To you, if to no one else, the baby was yours, was real, and will be missed forever by you, her mother.

You are loved. I wait with you as you grieve for the precious one who got away.

My love,

SPECIAL WORDS TO THE GRIEVING

Loss of Abusive Ex-Husband

Dearest Karen,

I just learned of your ex-husband's death when I spoke with your daughter Cindy. And while I know you and he have been divorced for years, still his death must have left you with a terrible mix of relief, fear, and anger.

Now you have the responsibility to comfort and care for Cindy's precious wounded heart, all because of the unfinished business her dad left behind.

I will never be able to understand the ugly word or act of *incest,* nor the fact that sometimes the perpetrator of sexual abuse seems to reach from the grave and continue the tormenting.

So today, tomorrow, and other tomorrows I'll be praying that God sends a special angel to walk *both* of you through the dark valley of adjustment. I will also pray that God's love and an angel of mercy will help you to resolve old conflicts, to heal the hemorrhaging wounds inflicted by Cindy's dad's actions, and to provide the help you need to walk out of the darkness into the sun, unblinking toward wholeness.

You and Cindy are in my prayers. May God bring healing into your hearts, quietly like the dawn.

My love,

Loss of a Loved One

Dear Marilyn,

When I talked to God about the loss of Susan and how concerned I am about your aching heart this morning, he assured me he is monitoring each heart blip and will be giving you the strength to go on. Then he whispered that I should keep on loving and praying for you. I thought, *That won't be difficult for me to do.*

And I shall do it.

Love,

~

Loss of a Loved One

Dearest Esther,

Yesterday at church [or wherever] I saw the tears forming in your eyes. Today I remembered someone's words, "Weeping is the lonely but necessary work of grief."

Personally, I believe weeping is best done together. Let me come over so I can cry with you.

My love,

Loss of a Loved One

Dearest Barbara,

You looked so wonderful when I saw you in the market [or wherever] that I wanted to rush right up to you and shout, "Wow, you look so great [or healthy, pretty, handsome]," but I didn't.

I don't want to be guilty of assuming that because you look great you are all right, all healed, and all better. You *may* not be. Certainly, it would be inappropriate of me to act as if you have finished with the pain of the grieving process when you might be smack-dab in the middle of it.

I don't want to add to your hurt. I know for a fact that we may never, ever stop missing our dearest loved ones. So I'll just tell you that when I saw you there in front of me, you had a serene beauty about you that was lovely, and I think I saw a halo of hope shining around your head, even though your heart must be so lonely [or sad, hurting, frustrated] for your dear Sam. I'll never forget the moment.

Love,

Loss of a Loved One

Dearest Barb and Bill,

We've been friends for 150 years (way back to good ol' Bob Jones Academy days), and throughout those years, we've laughed together and certainly shared a lot of joys!

Today we weep with you in Robert's death . . . and share your sorrows.

Forever friends,

About a Terminal Illness

Dear Nancy,

You were such a joy to talk with today, even if we were talking about your eighty-seven-year-old father, who's suffered his third heart attack and is presently fighting for his life.

How I pray that your times with him in the nursing home and with your family are a valuable memory-gathering experience. I also pray that you get enough good memories to tide you and your loved ones over— until you see your dad once again!

Grief, to my mind, is one of *the* most difficult emotions to deal with. But I sense you are very open to what the Lord would say to your heart and open also to the lessons he is gently teaching (which, of course, you will pass on to others!). And those lessons, as you know, will bring comfort to grieving spirits. In the meantime . . .

    You are loved and in my prayers,

Special Words
of Love

~

My dear Reader,

Often, when I hear people say they just *can't* say the words *I love you* aloud, I want to reply, "Okay, I understand that, but there are many different ways of letting your loved one *know* that you love her or him!"

Loving someone means learning how to talk about your love. It can be done, and it needs to be done because all of us have a deep desire to hear the life-sustaining words *I love you.*

If you feel that it's not in your nature or if you don't think it is necessary to say the words, then try touching the one you love. Sometimes a soft caress (not a crushing bear hug) and the loving look in your eyes speak louder than those three little words ever could.

Better yet, try writing down your love in your own handwriting.

Love notes need not always be your own original material. We are blessed with a wide world of poetry, prose, song lyrics, and great lines from plays, movies, TV. Beautiful or expressive lines written by someone else can suit your situation or spur on your imagination.

Remember Elizabeth Barrett Browning's famous love poem? It begins "How do I love thee? Let me count the ways." A bit farther down are the lines filled with both great beauty and practicality. She writes, "I love thee to the level of everyday's / Most quiet need . . ."

Then there are the ending lines that over the years have become the best of lovers' farewells:

> . . . I love thee with the breath,
> Smiles, tears, of all my life! — And if God
>   choose,
> I shall but love thee better after death.
> —*Sonnets from the Portuguese,* NO. XLIII

If we take just these brief lines and relate them to our own love relationships, or to an incident with a loved one, they become a very personal and original message of love.

Keep your eyes and ears open to phrases of love.

Since words sometimes can become trite or empty, we must learn to back these words with action. When I lost all my hair to chemo treatments, my cherisher announced, "With or without hair, I'll always love you." He followed that proclamation with a loving gesture or, as I call it, a touching action: He kissed every square inch of my bald, scruffy-looking head!

Later, to reemphasize his love, he brought me a tiny scented candle. Taped to the side of the candle base was a little blue Post-it with these new lyrics to an old song:

> You were scent for me.
> I was scent for you.
> And I'm convinced
> The angels must have scent you—
> And they scent you
> Just for me!

Corny or ridiculous? I don't think so! And neither will the one you love when you combine the words *I love you* with gentle touching-actions.

Sometimes *where* you put a love note is as important to the joy it gives as is *what* you say in it. Here are some ideas.

Tuck a note inside some clothing in a suitcase when your loved one is going away on a business trip, to summer camp, to the hospital, or just on a family visit. This is the unexpected *action* of love.

Insert love notes into your children's lunch bags or backpacks. These notes are a good way to reinforce your love to your kids, although they may not fully appreciate it until they grow up and have kids of their own. But it's worth the wait.

Put love notes (including compliments) under a loved

one's pillow. These notes to wife, husband, or children are heart-touching and give the feeling of intimacy.

Personally, I have discovered love notes all over the place, taped down or just lying in some of the following locations:

- on the stove: "You are the hottest little number in town," followed by an unmentionable illustration and an *I love you*.
- on the piano: "You are the music of my life."
- under the spoons in the silverware drawer: "Shall we spoon?"
- on the washing machine: "To the cleanest deal in the whole world!"
- on the bathroom mirror: "To the most beautiful wife in the history of the world."
- on the hall mirror: "Mirror, mirror on the wall, who's the fairest of them all? My wife! That's who."

In these tiny missives of loving words, you can be as serious or as whimsical as you choose. But I can tell you from experience, running across a semi-hidden note revives the magic of love for me. Perhaps it will for you as well!

Love,
Joyce

To My Husband

My dearest,

Once again you've reached into my soul in unforgettable and undeniable ways. It's like you to just *insist* on doing things up beautifully, and your generosity is beyond belief!

You made my birthday a joyous celebration. The tickets to the concert would have been more than enough, but dinner at the Shoreline restaurant—too much! It was an experience I'll always keep in my mind's eye . . . pictures and sounds and smells frozen in my memory—to be thawed out later.

Memories of seeing you in the restaurant, your beautiful wavy silver hair silhouetted against the darkening windows, those incredible blue eyes of yours looking lovingly at me, and oh, yes, the Texas sunset behind you!

My darling, it's so fun and wonderful to be married to you!

My love always,

SPECIAL WORDS OF LOVE

To My Husband

My darling Husband,

Bless you for giving me ten [twenty, thirty] extraordinary and superb years. During some of those years, we went through times that were:

emotionally scary, yet very exciting . . .

financially lean, yet richly rewarding . . .

mentally stressful, yet gloriously bonding . . .

spiritually challenging, yet faithfully strengthening . . .

But each year was the best, and even now, facing what we face, this year will be the best. The very best. That's the way things are between us.

The Rock of Gibraltar in our lives is our love for each other. I *do* love you. Happy anniversary, darling!

My love,

To My Husband

My darling Daniel,

It's a fact, an irrefutable fact, that I love you forever and beyond. In short, that means for all time!

My love,

To My Husband

My dear Cherisher,

No one can take your place in my heart. That's the absolute truth because you are the most beautiful gift God ever gave me.

Thank you for listening to me, for believing me, and for being on my side. It makes for a very strong and most romantic marriage.

I love you,

To My Husband

Alex, my dearest love,

I know I've been very "down" lately—the stress of what we are enduring gets to me every once in a while. (Well, maybe more than once in a while.) But I think you should know that, whether I'm up or down, you are my precious treasure and my most tender joy.

In short, you are the best reason in the whole world to stay alive. Up or down!

I love you,

To My Husband

Hello, love of my life,

It shouldn't surprise you that I think you're the most *wonderful* man in the history of the universe . . . or that you make me feel like the most *cherished* woman in the history of the universe. No, sir, it's not one bit surprising. Just true!

I love you,
Your wife

❧

To My Husband

Robert-honey,

About meals while I'm gone: In the fridge are sliced ham and cheese for sandwiches . . . cherry Jell-O for salad . . . grapes and celery for snacking . . . nonfat yogurt for dessert. In the pantry are canned soup and chili—and three bags of junk munchies.

If these staples don't do the trick, you can always starve as you wait for me to get home, three days from now, or go out to eat or whatever.

I haven't even left yet, and I already miss you. Do you miss me?

I love you,

To My Husband

Darling,

It was our friend and author Charlie Shedd who was brave enough to write about this charming note from his wife, Martha.

They had endured a rather lengthy verbal tussle, so Martha wrote this note and then left the house for a while. Martha's words are, to my way of thinking, absolutely classic of two people who love each other deeply but are temporarily at odds. Her note reads:

> Dear Charlie,
> I hate you.
>
> > Love,
> > Martha

Today, darling, this is the place where I am, because I'm still quite frustrated by our disagreement. But I'm counting on our love to sustain us and to make a bridge for us!

> My love,

To My Husband

My darling Matthew,

Yesterday, when I read someone's words about friendship being "a cozy shelter from life's stormy days," I thought, *Ah yes, that's quite true.*

Certainly our friendship is a cozy, all-sheltering umbrella, covering and protecting us from the rain of stormy days. Perhaps more so during these tornado days.

Our friendship doesn't *stop* the storms, the raging winds, or the torrential downpours of rain, but it does provide us a safe harbor where we can wait out the worst of the weather.

I love you, my darling. I believe in you. And I see clear sunrises and beautiful, storm-free sunsets in the future, because I know our love *and* our friendship will provide the best kind of shelter during the worst kind of storms.

And oh, by the way, I *love* sharing the umbrella with you!

My love,

To My Wife

My darling wife Joy,

Here I am, sitting in our living room, writing to *the* love of my life. I want to somehow do the impossible. I want to tell you how much I love you . . . what you mean to me . . . and how grateful I am for you. Of course, I'll be repeating myself, as I've said over and over again how much I appreciate these qualities in you, but they are as real to me as the air I breathe:

- your unparalleled beauty of body and soul
- your gift of giving beauty to so many people, places, and things
- your brilliance of mind
- your keen sensitivity
- your caring heart
- your creative genius so awesomely expressed in your writing, speaking, music, decorating, cooking, and ah yes, your wonderful love-making!

Beyond these qualities I admire and enjoy are the things that you do for me that just happen and keep on happening day in and day out, whether or not I say anything about them, like:

- washing and ironing my clothes
- pruning the shrubs and watering the plants
- having patience with my flaws and idiosyncrasies
- shopping for groceries
- enduring the sacrifices of being a one-car family.

My life is immeasurably enhanced by:

- the numerous ways you mother our children and grandchildren with thoughtful notes, creative gifts, care packages, cards, cartoons, and other items no one else but you would think of (and you do this for other people in our lives as well: parents, brothers, sisters, employees, special friends, and yes, often not-so-special but very needy friends);

- the thousand little ways you bring warmth, beauty, and variety into our lives—things that I may not notice at the time but that are a part of the ambience you create in our life together;

- your many prayers—the ones we pray together and all the ones I don't hear but know you are praying. (Believe me, your one-on-one friendship with God has saved my tail many times!)

Where does the list end? Like our love for each other, it never does. Sometimes I don't remember (or even know how) to acknowledge and thank you for *all* the particular ways you show your love to me . . . because they are innumerable. But I do love and admire you, my darling wife, with all that is in me!!

Happy Mother's Day,

To My Wife

My darling Sarah,

I wish I'd written the words on this beautiful card. God knows I've *felt* them, said them in my heart a million times.

It's been said before, but it's still true: I never knew
what it meant to be loved . . . until I was loved by you!

Happy anniversary, and I'm counting on many, many
more!

My love,

To My Wife

My darling Helen,

Here it is in a nutshell:

I love you, our marriage, our children, our grandchildren, and our mission in life!

There. I said it, and I'm glad.

Your loving husband,

To My Loved One

My darling love,

You and I know love is far, far more than just a warm,
fuzzy buzz around the heart or eating chocolate chip
cookies together.

We know that keeping love alive and healthy through
the years *demands* that we extend to each other large help-
ings of patience, goodwill, understanding, and grace on

the marriage plate. We also know that it takes lots of work to keep good-sized portions in front of us, to keep the flow of communication running smoothly.

But after all that hard work, then maybe, just maybe, we'll sit down to enjoy the wonderful, warm, fuzzy buzzes . . . and together we'll eat really good chocolate chip cookies!

Until then, like the Seven Dwarfs in *Snow White*, we'll whistle while we work . . .

My love,

To My Loved One

Dearest one,

The heart is always in the process of unraveling or entwining.

Unraveling is terribly sad.

Entwining is joyously wonderful.

So today I send this note in the high hopes of *entwining* your heart with mine . . . forever and ever!

My love,

To My Loved One
(A Note Placed at . . .
[fill in])

Yoohoo, darling,

Hello, down there.

Can you see me?

No?

Well, look up.

That's right!

See . . . I'm in your balcony, cheering you on and waving my jacket above my head for extra emphasis. I don't even care if others think I'm making a fool of myself. I'm going to keep on yelling over the balcony railing, so you'll know I'm not only *for* you, I'm *with* you all the way. I'm forever on *your* side!

And oh, yes, no one can shove me out of your balcony. I'm staying right up here . . . regardless and always!

My love,

To My Loved One

My dearest love,

Sometimes I'm absolutely sure you and I *can* and *will* stay this much in love *forever*!

103

SPECIAL WORDS OF LOVE

But then—maybe even the next day—a verbal storm comes up, and the tranquility of our relationship is severely threatened. And I wonder, what happened to yesterday's love?

Quickly though, I remember that even when the storms do rage, you and I seem to be able, eventually, to catch each other's hand and race to a safe shelter. Over and over we have survived the howling wind and the downpour of rain.

So I guess it's true, at least for us, that you and I will stay in love forever.

Storm or no storm.

I love you,

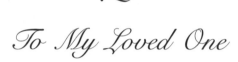

To My Loved One

My dearest Robert,

My heart goes with you today as you keep this rather delicate yet arduous meeting with your friend Ron.

I'll be asking the Lord to strengthen your heart continually for this task of love that you must carry out with Ron.

The outcome of your time together is not really as important as your being his friend and Christian brother.

Please know that my spirit, my love, and my prayers go with you. I love you so much—much more than you know.

My love,

To My Loved One

My dearest,

Whenever I try to write down my love for you, I don't seem to be instantly creative. It bothers me, because I love you so dearly.

Then this morning I saw a cartoon of a woman at her desk, just holding on to her pen. And her thoughts read:

> I have big concepts, but
> I have such little words!

Aha! There I am—but I'm sure you'll understand. Although our love is a *big concept,* my heart can come up with only three little words—I love you!

Truly,

To My Loved One

My darling Cherisher,

As fun and invigorating as lunch with friends can be, still my favorite thing is to have lunch, dinner, snacks, or just a root beer float with you. Alone and together!

Isn't this remarkable? Here in this world, with all its billions of human souls, nothing touches, nothing reaches, nothing satisfies me quite like being alone and together with you!

Too bad, sweetie—this means you're stuck with me forever, 'cause I ain't leavin'!

My love,

Special Words
for Difficult Relationships

~

My dear Reader,

As much as I don't like to think, much less admit, that loved ones and friends can experience difficult and even shattering times in their relationships with each other . . . it *does* happen. And it happens, perhaps, more often than we think or know about.

We Christians, our families, and our brothers and sisters in the family of God are in no way immune to the sad and lonely "trauma" of difficult relationships involving the people closest to us. It is possible to experience everything from the mildly disturbing cracks that appear from time to time to the seemingly irreparable hopelessness of a completely broken relationship.

So the question is not, "Will there be any difficult relationships in my life?" But rather, "When difficult relationships *do* materialize, how will I cope?" How will I bring healing out of pain, and how will I survive these awful conflicts?

What comes to mind first is that as a Christian woman I should take every reasonable step to resolve troubled relationships. No one should neglect or overlook the opportunities for reconciliation with the people we call family and friends. I'm confident that if we do try for understanding and aim for fixing what's broken, oftentimes the relationships can be healed and the soul-needs of others, as well as ourselves, will be met.

"But," I hear you say, "what if all my peace-making efforts, my loving gestures of care, and my sincerely felt and stated apologies go unheeded or just fall miserably short and fail in achieving any kind of reconciliation? What then?"

I know you are thinking about a relationship you once had with a person (or persons) when your friendship broke and you moved into a very different kind of relationship. And the name *friend* changed to the name *enemy*.

A number of years ago I was shocked when I realized that it was entirely possible, even probable, for us as Christians to have real flesh-and-blood antagonists, or as Christ called them, enemies. No, I'm not talking about Satan or his followers but about people in our family or church or Bible study group or wherever. I mean those people who, by definition, oppose and contend against each other. I'm referring to those who once were friends but over the course of time, because of a number of difficult circumstances, differing opinions and choices, opposing theological viewpoints, or whatever, the friendships gradually faded or perhaps suddenly snapped like a small brittle twig on an icy winter's day. No amount of reconciliatory overtures has brought resolution, and nothing seems to restore or revive the once healthy relationships.

Over and over again, a suffering brother or sister in Christ has stood before me, filled with deep anguish and bewilderment, and asked, "How could she say such a terrible thing about me?" "How could he do this to me?" "She is my oldest friend. . . . I've talked, pleaded, and prayed about our relationship, but nothing changes." "All I know is that he's not my friend anymore . . . so what is he to me now?"

In this context, the mere mention of the word *enemy* frightens me. But the truth is that whether we are fearful or just theologically uncomfortable in acknowledging it, the presence of enemies within our families and in the body of Christ is a reality.

I'm grateful that the Bible addresses this thorny problem. Enemies are mentioned hundreds of times in the Old Testament and in more than two dozen passages in the New Testament.

What I find amazing, though, is this: Jesus didn't say we *wouldn't* have enemies; he simply told us how we should respond and react, what our attitudes and prayers should be, and how to deal with these very difficult relationships.

Jesus said:

> Listen, all of you. Love your enemies. Do good
> to those who hate you. Pray for the happiness

SPECIAL WORDS FOR DIFFICULT RELATIONSHIPS

of those who curse you; implore God's blessing on those who hurt you (Luke 6:27–28).

When we take Jesus' words seriously and admit that we do have a few antagonists and *beloved* enemies in our lives, I believe we are more likely to find ultimate solutions. And when we actively identify and deal with the difficult relationships in our conscious minds rather than submerging them inside of us by denial, we are well on our way to spiritual, mental, emotional, and even physical wholeness.

Coming out of denial and delineating who is and who is not a "practicing" friend, understanding that a long-time friendship is over and may not be reinstated except in heaven one day, and believing that our Savior made a provision of grace for us *and* our beloved enemies can be a giant step in moving on without bitterness. Best of all, accepting these realities can provide an enormous healing for the broken, bruised, and battered parts of our souls.

Only a loving and merciful God would think of such a great solution for the enemies in our lives: "Love them, and pray for them." And so it is with God's healing words ringing in our hearts that you and I can set down on paper notes to the people in our lives who are separated from us by broken relationships.

Once in a blue moon, or on a fifth Tuesday of the month, when our backs are up against the wall, when our patience is exhausted, or when our depression has gathered momentum, it will be time to write someone a note that is difficult but necessary for our well-being or sanity.

It's a note that closes a door rather than opens one, but it's a necessary note nonetheless.

You'll be the first to know when the moment has arrived. So I wish you courage and suggest that you be careful about burning *all* your bridges. Leave at least one intact—you may need it someday.

You may or may not want to send your notes. But I suspect that even realizing who is a friend and who is a beloved enemy, treating each of them as Christ has admonished, and writing out your hurts can well make a significant difference in your feelings of helplessness and hopelessness and perhaps restore your own spiritual, emotional, and physical wellness as you learn to live with your brothers and sisters in Christ.

Love,
Joyce

Dear Sam,

I am stunned by your letter informing me that you will no longer represent me as my attorney. Being a single mother, the mere fact of losing your services is overwhelming, but your reasons are even more devastating.

The D.U.I. charge looked terrible, especially since I am a Christian and so active in our church. But the truth is, I really had not had any alcohol. And when I got that call from the baby-sitter, I forgot that I had just taken one pain killer. The effects didn't hit me until I was already

SPECIAL WORDS FOR DIFFICULT RELATIONSHIPS

on the way home . . . and then that awful accident happened . . . followed by all the rest, with no one believing my explanation.

Sam, I know that since you are on the board of elders, defending me might put you in a bad light. But now is when I need your help most, because you are both an excellent attorney and a Christian brother who should believe and support me.

How can you, as you said, "for the sake of Christian testimony" drop me now? What's more important—the way things look or the way they really happened?

I am writing to you so you can think all this over before we talk. I will call you tomorrow.

Warmly,
Lisa

My dear Loretta,

I remember the scene so clearly. I was in our bedroom talking about you with Robert . . . no, actually I was ranting and raving and sobbing my heart out about the latest painful experience between you and me.

With tears scalding my face, I cried, "How can she be so cruel? I know that in her position she can do virtually anything she wishes. But we were so close for so long! Our families went on picnics together. And we worked side by side. Loretta is my friend . . ."

At that precise moment, as the word *friend* was still

rolling off my tongue, deep inside my spirit I heard, "I don't think so." And then I thought, *I'm calling her by the wrong name. Our relationship has become so antagonistic that we are now literally at war with each other.*

I stared at Robert. Then, half proclaiming and half questioning, I said, "Loretta and I are no longer friends? We are enemies?"

While I was still digesting this saddening realization, the unspoken thoughts mirrored on my face were begging my husband to tell me what in the world I was going to do about Loretta.

Calmly, Robert gently said, "Darling, we know what Jesus said to do about our enemies. Does the fact that Loretta used to be your friend change what he said?"

Good grief! I thought. *He could have lived a long time without hitting me with that proof text!*

It took me a number of days to work through the realization that you and I really have become enemies. But when I did, Loretta, I experienced the beginnings of healing in my emotions.

Before, your actions toward me made no sense whatsoever because I viewed them as coming from a friend. Now they make complete sense, and I know exactly what I must do if our friendship is ever to be restored.

I must ". . . love you, and bless you, and pray for you."

And that is what I am doing right now—and will continue doing so until we are on the same side again.

In his love,

SPECIAL WORDS FOR DIFFICULT RELATIONSHIPS

Dear Sandra,

I have been told about your critical remarks concerning me. I'm saddened because I'm aware of how you use your public appearances to criticize men and women. At least I know I'm not the only one who has felt your rejection and your public renouncements.

I believe it was Nancy Reagan who once said, "You get over being surprised [by criticism], but it still hurts."

Sandra, since you are very involved in a public ministry and still relatively young, the day may dawn when someone (a friend or a peer) decides to smudge and tarnish or even attack *your* credibility or *your* character. Or some self-appointed critic may cast a negative judgment about *your* personhood or *your* work. I pray this doesn't happen . . . but unfortunately these kinds of critics go with the territory.

When someone misrepresents you, it will devastate your spirit and your feelings of self-worth. It's funny, but people think that being in the public limelight is all fun and games and looks so glamorous, when in reality it puts one in a very vulnerable place and is often quite scary. So I offer these few lines of counsel gleaned from dealing with my own wounds over someone's painfully cutting comments.

I know that when we are criticized (especially publicly) we begin to doubt most everything we've ever done, we are convinced our antagonists are right, and we experience a dark pervading kind of hopelessness about God's plan for our lives and our mission statement. We do this

114

even if we *know* the things being said are not accurate or true.

I pray that should you ever experience these doubts, that is, when you reach the point where criticism overwhelms you . . . that you will take heart and comfort from this very old eight-line poem:

Sweet Remembrance

Let fate do her worst; there are relics of joy,
Bright dreams of the past, which she cannot
    destroy;
And which come in the night-time of sorrow
    and care,
To bring back the features that joy used to
    wear.
Long, long be my heart with such memories
    filled,
Like the vase in which roses have once been
    distilled;
You may break, you may ruin the vase, if you
    will,
But the scent of the roses will hang round it
    still.

—T. Moore*

---

* Mrs. J.S.F. Lunt, ed., *Forget-Me-Not, or The Philopene.* (Lowell: Nathaniel L. Dayton, 1846).

SPECIAL WORDS FOR DIFFICULT RELATIONSHIPS

It's the last two lines that mean the most to me, Sandra. And they have helped me to be forgiving of your and others' critical words. Maybe these lines will minister to you and give you hope someday in the future when you've just been unfairly or unjustly criticized by another sister in Christ. But beyond that, I do pray for your outstanding ministry, and I know I can trust God's mercy for both of us. And I do.

In his love,

Dear Mrs. Anderson,

You may be surprised to hear from me after all these years, but the other day your name came up in a conversation I had with my beautiful and now grown up daughter. As we recalled and reassessed the damaging aspects of your relationship with her (and me) we discovered that both of us had some difficult and unresolved business with you.

Years ago when you were my daughter's fifth-grade teacher, you verbally stripped her of self-esteem by calling her stupid. You made a big mistake! But when you stood her up in front of her classmates, ridiculing and humiliating her day after day, you went way beyond a "big mistake." And I will never understand why, in all our many teacher-parent conferences and conversations, you repeatedly *denied* that there was *any* problem with her—either scholastically or personally. So I kept her in your class with the hope that it really was all right. That was *my* big mistake.

In one short semester you took an eager, "I can't wait to get to school" ten-year-old and crushed her spirit and self-esteem with your insults and threats. You turned her into someone who *believed* she was a failure completely without value who passionately hated going to school.

You also did something else in the process . . . you betrayed the professional community of gifted, conscientious, and caring men and women who *are* committed to the excellence of teaching in our schools. And I can't help but wonder how many other children's self-esteem, during other years, you damaged.

By the time my daughter finished the fifth grade with you, she adamantly refused to *ever* go back to school. I remember that during the long summer that year, all I could do, as I watched the terror in her eyes deepen as the fall term drew near, was to pray for a miracle.

Did you know that miracles still happen, Mrs. Anderson? Well, they do! In fact, God really intervened. Somehow Miss Lockhart was assigned to be my daughter's teacher for the sixth grade.

Miracle of miracles! The nourishing and nurturing care Miss Lockhart lavished on my child poured over her and began to turn her emotional and educational life around. That whole year with Miss Lockhart slowly transformed a drop-out wannabe into an eager-to-learn student once again.

As my daughter and I continued our conversation about her year in your class, I began to realize I failed to give you any respect, understanding, or grace during that time.

It occurs to me now that maybe you were unaware (somehow) of just how hurtful your role as a teacher that year was to a student. Perhaps nowadays you are no longer the insensitive kind of teacher you were that year. Because both of us are Christians, I should have grasped sooner the truth of Proverbs 11:17: "Your own soul is nourished when you are kind; it is destroyed when you are cruel." I see that now.

I do want to say, whether you are still teaching or not, I wish that you would take to heart the apostle Paul's words: "Whatever you do, do it with kindness and love" (1 Cor. 16:14).

And in spite of the pain you caused my daughter and me, I really am grateful for the lessons we both learned from you and from the relationship we once shared.

May God bless you and give you joy
as you serve in his name,

My dear Mother [Father],

For years I have wanted—no, yearned and longed for—your approval. Just a small pat on the back, a quiet smile, or some tiny gesture from you that I'd "done good." But I wonder if I'm not wasting my years in frustration and in endless hoping for what probably is never going to be.

So, because I do know that I am basically a good person, a loving daughter [son], and that I must give my attention to my own journey to be the woman [man] I think God wants me to be to myself, my husband [wife], and my children, I'm not going to wait for your approval any longer. I won't agonize inside for a small gesture of love from you. I will not set aside hours or even moments of wishful thinking about what "could have been" for us. I am closing out these painful chapters in my life.

Someday you might have a change of heart, a reversal, or a turnaround of thought, or you might even transpose some of your attitudes. Such a change would be wonderful, and I would welcome communication between us. But for now I have to, as psychologists say, move on with my mind *and* my heart and tell you I can no longer hope, expect, or even wait for change.

I will always love you. You are my mother [father], and I pray things will go well for you.

Your daughter [son],

My dear ones,

Since I do not want to be part of any unpleasantness or create an unwanted stir, I feel it's best if we don't celebrate Christmas with you this year.

This is not what I want. I would prefer to be there with everyone, but last year all that transpired was the usual and terrible arguments between us. There was very little joy and even less celebration.

Maybe at a later time we will be able to put aside our differences, at least for a little while, and just be together as a family. I surely hope so, and that's my heart's prayer.

Until then, I send my love,

Dear Dad,

I am writing this note on behalf of my sister. She didn't ask me to write nor does she know of this letter. But I must write to you about the need for making amends with her.

You say the abuse never happened, so it's your word against hers. But it looks to me as if you are saying that she made this whole thing up. Or worse, that she's lying.

Dad, in pretending you're not guilty, you are simply carrying on with the abuse, only in a different way. I'd *love* to believe that the sexual abuse never happened, but there is too much evidence to the contrary.

There will never be any bridges built between you and [name of sister] until you tell her the words she longs to hear from you: "I'm sorry." That's all, Dad—just those two little words. It won't change or erase what you did to her, but it will help her take an enormous step forward into the wellness she deserves. I know you can do it . . .

Your son,

Dear Dr. Wilson,

It has been more than a year since I left your practice and have been under the care of my new doctor.

Do you remember that during our very first consultation together I explained that I wanted you to tell me the good and the bad news in a straightforward manner? You assured me that you understood and would level with me.

Then we talked of the types of treatments that would begin that day. But within two weeks, I was shocked to realize that *most* of what you had told me was vague, evasive, and either did not in any way apply to my case or proved to be untrue.

After a while, I realized also that to you I was a nameless, faceless patient. Number 5 in the ten or fifteen people you saw each day. If I asked you a question or told you what I'd read or heard from a breast surgeon friend of mine, you impatiently responded that I was being "ridiculous"; a couple of times you said that what I had read or heard was just plain "stupid." And then, when I asked you another question, you pronounced me "severely clinically depressed" and prescribed Prozac.

At that point I crossed a line. With my husband's and my family's support, I finally drew the boundaries and refused to go any farther with you. It was very liberating for me. I'm sure that the move out of your care and offices finally enabled me to begin the delayed healing process.

Why am I writing this now, after all this time? It's really very simple: While most of your patients have life-threatening diseases, we are very individualistic in our battles. We are not mere numbers on your charts or daily

SPECIAL WORDS FOR DIFFICULT RELATIONSHIPS

schedules. We are men, women, sons, daughters, husbands, wives, and grandparents who do *not* need your judgment or evaluation of our mental, moral, or emotional conditions. We *do* need your individually thought-through expertise in our treatment, for we are real people with real, life-threatening diseases.

Also, I'm writing this note to you because I don't believe it's too late. You still have a great opportunity not only to talk to your patients about their illness but also to listen to them, to believe them, and to take them seriously enough to be on their side. I believe that you could still be the physician and healer that the Hippocratic oath has set as a hallmark for men and women like you who practice medicine.

Respect goes two ways. It cannot merely go from me, the patient, to you, the doctor; it must flow mutually between us. In fact, *both* of us are, first and foremost, human beings, who should be respected and treated with grace and dignity.

Do this, Dr. Wilson, and I believe your measure as a physician-healer will be greater than you ever dreamed.

Sincerely,

Dear Pastor, Church Board, and Staff,

I'm writing this note not just for me but for several people in our church who are calling out for help and who feel they're drowning and going down for the third time. You know them all as they are a part of our church family.

For me, it's a divorce; for Clara and Jim, it's a son who's gay and now has AIDS; for Jill and Mike, it's infidelity; for Joan and Bob, it's a business in bankruptcy, coupled with a fire their son started that destroyed their home; for Sarah and Ted, it's their daughter's pregnancy and subsequent abortion; for Robert, our gifted minister of music, it's his homosexuality; for Cynthia, it's her husband's incest with their daughter; for Sharon, it's being a single parent . . . I could go on, but these are the ones who have spoken to me about writing this letter. We are all in your congregation, and we have one other trait in common: We are each in the midst of a terrible crisis. Our panic buttons have been pushed. Repeatedly.

I feel that your responses to me in these matters are unbelievable and shattering. I am stunned. And so are the others I mentioned.

We came to you looking for help and healing, praying for God's love to minister to our brokenness. We found, tragically, that instead of reaching out to us as forgiven sinners, you have responded to us in these ways:

- You have made set-in-concrete pronouncements and iron clad judgments without facts or compassion about Clara and Jim, Joan and Bob, and others.

- You have taken cruel vengeance against some of us even though you preach "Vengeance is mine, saith the Lord." You have forbidden Sharon to teach Sunday school and have refused to talk with Sarah and Ted's daughter, yet you constantly preach about how "New Testament" you are.
- You have decided who is and who is not disqualified from any Christian endeavor or ministry. You have made it clear as to who is or is not forbidden to worship or fellowship with other church members.

I have to ask, Where is the grace or the love of Christ in these responses of yours? Have you lost the basic agenda of the vision and mission that you so often claim to be carrying out?

Look around you, dear men and women of God, and see the wounded sinners at your door. Hear our cries for help. Please. I have faith that God will show you how to be a part of our forgiveness and healing, and what you can do about our broken and shattered souls.

If we who are in the midst of crisis cannot come to you for help toward the wellness of our souls, where shall we go? And where, just tell me where, will we see the face of Christ if we don't see him in *your* faces?

We are broken beyond belief,

Dear Dr. Wilson,

As you know, for the past six months during my chemo treatments I've been under your care. My husband and I thank you for your medical expertise and skills on my behalf.

However, for some time now, I have felt it would be appropriate for me to seek out a second or third opinion. I have now done that, and I've decided to put myself under the care of another oncologist.

I would appreciate it if you would kindly forward all my medical records, at your earliest convenience, to Doctor George W. Smith at St. David's Hospital here in Austin, Texas.

Again, thank you for your help in the past, and I wish you success in your practice in the future as you deal with cancer patients and their families.

Sincerely,

Special Words to "Balcony People"

~

My dear Reader,

In most of our relationships we have two very basic and distinctive types of people. They are light-years apart from each other in how they think, give advice, or respond to our hearts and minds.

There is the "Basement Person," who is at best our critical *evaluator* and is not terribly concerned or burdened with our state of emotional well-being and, at the worst, is capable of shattering even the strongest tenets of our character and integrity. The fact is that the presence of a Basement Person in our lives is very disruptive and often quite painful. That's a sad reality of life.

But here's the good news. There is the "Balcony Person," who by experience, by education in the school of suffering, and by the wisdom gleaned from life is our *affirmer*. Balcony People "light up my life," as the song lyrics say. They are people who take delight in honoring one another (a rare commodity these days). Balcony People not only love us but have great respect for us. They listen to us with their ears and hear us with their hearts.

In my book *Balcony People* (Austin: Balcony Publishing, 1984), I wrote:

> When others discern the good, the noble, the honorable, and the just tenets of our character (no matter how minuscule they may be) and then proceed to tell us how they admire those traits, we feel visible. We begin to "see" ourselves and our worth. We feel nurtured and nourished, but mostly we feel loved.

So now it's our turn. We can write notes of love and encouragement to the people in our balcony, to those dear souls who are cheering us on and who love us "as is." We can also write to people who are hurting or who are just slogging wearily along in life, and we can be affirmers to them . . . real Balcony People to them! Give it a try! Who knows what a "Balcony Note" can do to lift and love another spirit? In the meantime, I'm in your balcony, cheering you on.

Love,
Joyce

My dear Sharon,

I know I live 1,500 miles away, but I want you to look up into the balcony of your mind.

See me there? Way up in the grandstand?

I'm the one waving my coat over my head, making an absolute fool out of myself, and yelling, "See that girl down there on the field? Well, she's the greatest, and I love her. . . . Isn't she terrific?"

I'm in your balcony forever! Carry on. We need all the wonderful people like you we can get!

My love from the balcony,

Dearest one,

On such a stormy, rainy day as was yesterday, I loved the fact that your reality-based yet cheerful attitude spread over me like an umbrella of hope. (You took the edge off my panic.)

When it's a cloudless, sunny day, you remind me to be grateful, and then we tap-dance on the table together!

So when it comes to Balcony People, on a scale from 1 to 10, you are definitely a 12. And I think, oh, my, how the world needs more people exactly like you!

Love,

Greetings, dearest Margaret,

Speaking of friends (and this is especially true of *our* friendship), Henry David Thoreau said it best when he wrote:

> Friends cherish each other's hopes.
> They are kind to each other's dreams.

Thank you, dear Balcony Person, for cherishing my hopes and being kind about my dreams of a new life with John. You believed our marriage not only would work, but also that it would really sing. And as to my dreams . . . well, you never once put them down. You were a true friend to us at a time when just about *everyone* else thought John and I were a nightmare team! Turns out, you were right, and *they* were wrong!

Now, on the eve of our tenth year together, our anniversary is sweetened a bit because of the memories we have about you and Thoreau's dear words!

You are loved by us,

Dearest Aunt Louise,

This morning when I read the words in James 1:17 about every good, even perfect, gift coming from God, I thought, *That statement certainly applies to Aunt Louise!*

You are truly a gift to me from God, and I love your being in my balcony! Maybe that's because you bring out the very best in me. . . . Do I do that for you? I surely hope so!

Your loving niece,

Dearest MaryAnn and Kevin,

It was remarkably special to see you both again . . . even though the time at lunch was so brief.

I realized once more why heaven *is* heaven for one of a thousand reasons: In heaven we won't keep running out of time!

Until then (when we're in heaven, I mean), I'll take whatever time I can carve out to be with you two Balcony People . . . even if it's just for lunch or for *half* of a lunch!

You are loved,

My dearest daughter Laurie,

Even when you were little, you had the rare and beautiful gift of a stunningly sensitive and compassionate heart. You possessed, and still do possess, the extraordinary ability to see *beyond* someone's eyes, words—even actions. Amazing! Perhaps you developed that gift, in part, because of your serious hearing impairment, but whatever the reason, darling, you've got quite a gift!

SPECIAL WORDS TO "BALCONY PEOPLE"

I remember the first time I became aware of the way you intensely read people's faces in determining what they are feeling. You were about four years old, standing quietly beside me at the kitchen sink. I was peeling potatoes for dinner, unaware that I was frowning. Suddenly your tiny, precious voice broke through my concentration.

"Mommie, are you happy to me?"

Surprised, I bent over, hugged you, and assured you that, yes, I was "happy to you." I asked, "Honey, what makes you think I'm not?"

Your simple answer, "Because you don't *look* happy!" alerted my heart for the first time to the specialness of your gift.

Down through the years, even now that you're grown, you're the one person in a million who can silently probe beyond faces, actions, or explanations to see what really matters. In short, you notice all the little things others miss, because you have a sensitive heart.

Best of all, darling, I'm so glad you're in my "balcony." You're one of those rare people in my world who sees beyond and behind the dark circles under my eyes, the red nose from crying, the frowns of concentration, or the cover-up mask and demeanor I wear when I'm feeling absolutely rotten . . . and always you get right down to the nitty-gritty of what's *really* going on inside me!

Am I grateful for this incredible gift of yours . . . this gift you give so unsparingly to me and to everyone else you know?

Are you kidding?

Of course, I am! I pray God kisses your forehead with his blessings because you've given this gift so freely and so compassionately! And not so incidentally . . . never forget I'm in *your* "balcony," always and regardless.

Your loving and grateful,
Mom XXOO

My dearest Stepdaughter,

I just know in my heart of hearts that when God put you on this earth before I even knew you, he had some very special plans in mind . . . like our friendship.

Do you think God does that on purpose? I do, because he knows just who is absolutely perfect for this very moment in our lives. Just who we need and just who will fill in for one of his angels!

So, dear one, your tenderness to me is a treasure, and your caring for me makes the difference. What a Balcony Woman you are!

You are such a blessing in my life!

My love always,

Dearest Andrew,

Today I decided to be a Balcony Person to you, and so I made out a list. Here are a few random thoughts that

SPECIAL WORDS TO "BALCONY PEOPLE"

happened inside my head when I thought of you, dear Andrew.

You are a blessing from God in my life.

You don't force your ideas on me; . . . you simply pull back the cobwebs of my own mind and let me see what special ideas just might just be there already.

You remind me, oh, so sweetly, to look at the larger picture, to stick to my mission statement, and to focus on what is truly significant and real in life.

You come and stay with me when I'm sick or when my heart is bruised.

You are a man of steely principles tempered by gentle wisdom and compassion. I pray these qualities are rubbing off on me.

I want you to know that—*always, forever, and beyond*—I am in your "balcony," cheering you on! I already know you are in mine. Stay there. Please.

Love,

My dear Cynthia,

You know *why* you're so special, not only to me but to others? Well, it's because you've developed an incredible gift: the gift of listening.

As I was thinking about you and your precious gift, I realized we probably don't learn or grow a whole lot from the things we *say*, but when we listen, it opens up a whole world of learning and growth. Listening even develops the lost art of compassion.

The way *you* listen is the finest way of all! It is spirit-enriching, and you, dear one, are the best in the world at it!

Thank you for all the years you've been in others' balconies and in mine, listening to and hearing our hearts so clearly! In heaven your crown will be incredibly heavy because of all the jewels God's going to put on it for your gift of listening to others!

My love,

My dearest Julia,

Your name crossed my mind today, and so I thought I'd jot down these thoughts to you.

I really pray that you take a fair amount of pleasure in reading this note and in knowing that some years ago during my divorce when the only thing I could believe was that no one, absolutely no one, cared about me, you, dear, sweet Julia, wrote me many a life-saving letter, which gave me a ton of unfettered grace and love.

Remember? No? Well, it just so happens that I've kept every one of your letters all this time. In one very special letter, at a time when I was at my lowest level of depression, you wrote:

SPECIAL WORDS TO "BALCONY PEOPLE"

I don't know why your divorce has happened, or for that matter, why or how painful things happen in life as they do . . . but I believe and trust your judgment and your right-standing with God. I also believe you *must* have had good cause and many legitimate reasons for the decisions you reached.

See why it's easy for me to think of you? Bless your darling heart, dear Balcony Woman!

My love and gratitude always,

Dearest Bettye,

Remember when we sat together in choir—and talked and laughed entirely too much? Well, today I found myself humming one of those choir numbers. It was an arrangement of the chorus "Let the Beauty of Jesus Be Seen in Me."

And I thought, *It's true. God's beauty can really work and be seen in us.* It can shine, like it did on your face, as I recall.

In fact, I have seen the beauty of Jesus not only on your face but in you in so many special ways. And today the memories of your beauty led me back to this passage of Scripture in 2 Corinthians 3:18:

But we Christians have no veil over our faces;
we can be mirrors that brightly reflect the glory
of the Lord. And as the Spirit of the Lord
works within us, we become more and more
like him.

Yes, that's you, Bettye. I'm always in your balcony,
cheering you on.

Love,

My dear Mrs. Buttons,

I know why my daughter came by to see you several times in the past years. She had to let you know how grateful both of us are for your encouraging words and your kind, nurturing, and loving teaching ways with her. In my heart and hers you were a G.S.T. (God-Sent Teacher).

Neither of us has ever forgotten the crushed little girl who more than reluctantly dragged herself into your sixth-grade classroom. Her terrible experiences in the fifth grade, coupled that same year with the deaths of her infant brother and her beloved grandmother, left her mind spent and her emotions shattered.

But you made all the difference, and we'll never, ever forget you, dear teacher.

Thank you for being in my daughter's "balcony" and for cheering her on through one of the most difficult peri-

SPECIAL WORDS TO "BALCONY PEOPLE"

ods of her young life. Somehow, you completely understood this verse in Proverbs, which says, "Anxious hearts are very heavy but a word of encouragement does wonders!" (Prov. 12:25).

I'm sure there will be an extra star in your crown in heaven, and if you look closely, you'll probably see my daughter's face reflected in it. Bless you!

My loving gratitude, dear Balcony Woman!

Special Words
to the Hurting

~

My dear Reader,

You already know what note is absolutely the most difficult to write—don't you? It is the note to someone who is breaking apart at the seams. It may be to a loved one, a family member, or a friend when he or she is suffering great pain—either physically, emotionally, or worse, both.

When it's time, or past time, to reach out by writing to that hurting person, we all become excellent procrastinators. Our rationale convinces us that the task is beyond our writing skills and too formidable to even try to tackle. So we put it off. Besides, what can we say that will relate to this person—when our own pain levels are presently so minor in comparison?

I believe it's urgent for all of us to understand that no matter how qualified or unqualified we feel about writing notes to the hurting or how easy or hard the task, notes to the hurting may well be the most important communication we will ever set our pens to write.

When it comes to the multitudes of people who hurt, our world seems to be at critical mass proportions. Hurting people are on the six o'clock news, they fill our newspapers and magazines, they own or rent the house next door or a few blocks down, and they work beside us on the job. They belong to our church, sing in the choir, preach from the pulpit, or teach our Sunday school class. They attend school with our children, they shop at the same grocery store as we do, and some of them are even our own family members—living under our roofs or in a home of their own.

But make no mistake, *all* of us have experienced, are experiencing, or will experience the agony of pain. There are all types and descriptions, levels and magnitudes of pain that bore like dreaded parasites into almost everyone I know—including me. Whether we admit the pain or deny it, whether we openly discuss it or never mention it, whether we endure in silence or disappear down the dark shaft of depression, the suffering from pain is almost always with us and often has the power to devastate the human spirit.

Hence the urgent need for a handwritten note.

We may think that our note to a hurting person is not of vital importance, but I know from receiving them that we who are in the press of pain prize those brief words on paper from someone who has taken the time and cared enough to write.

"But," I can hear you say wearily, "what can I put on paper that's not going to sound glib or trite? And what hasn't been said a thousand times before?" Or, "What words, though they come sincerely from my heart, and are based on good intentions, are inadvertently going to add weight to the already unbearable pain, simply by an error in my choice of words?"

These are all valid concerns; we don't want to say the *wrong* words, but never underestimate the healing power of one human being caring for another.

People who are hurting are, in a real sense, isolated in an emotional intensive-care ward. If you've ever been there, I don't have to tell you that the ICU experience is extremely lonely. So our written note may be the only way of reaching in, touching his or her life, and giving a moment's relief from pain and loneliness.

However, because the circumstances and human factors involved in our own journey with pain widely differ, we must not take it for granted that we completely "know and understand" the depths of another's suffering. So it's probably a good idea to admit from the outset that while we cannot fully understand the hurt, we *do* care.

Writing a care-note simply starts by thinking back about what comforted us when we were suffering. It means recalling things about the person we're writing to—what he or she said, did, or gave to us in the past. It also means focusing on the sole mission and ultimate goal of our message—which is to try, as best we can, to give the hurting one the essence of comfort and the ambiance of solace.

We hope the written words to the suffering will fly off the page and wrap like a blanket around their shoulders and hearts so they can, for just a few moments, feel and absorb the healing warmth of God's loving care and ours.

Love,

Joyce

Divorce

My dear Shirley,

Isn't it strange that even though your divorce was final some time ago the pain continues? It's a little like the bunny with the Eveready battery—the pain just goes on and on and on!

It was Shakespeare who gave us this line, "What wound did ever heal but by degrees?" (*Othello*).

So I'm prayerfully hoping for a whole bunch of "degrees" of healing for your broken heart and shattered spirit. I won't be so callous and insensitive as to think because you *appear* "whole and hearty" that you are all "healed up." Oh, no, healing is *rarely* instantaneous.

I'm committed to praying for the various ways God's healing will spread, by degrees, over your mind, body, and soul. And I'll try not to be too impatient.

My love,

Divorce

My dear Matthew,

It's no wonder you feel as if you've lost everything. No wonder that right now you feel as if nothing will ever be right again—nothing will ever make you smile, give you joy, or allow that elusive word *hope* to bloom again.

I have no instant answers, no magic solutions, and no treasures to replace the ones you've lost, but I can offer you this tiny thimbleful of hope. I wrote your name, Matthew, in the margin of my Bible beside these words:

> The thought of my pain, my hopelessness, is
> bitter poison.
> I think of it constantly and my spirit is
> depressed.
> Yet hope returns when I remember this one
> thing:
> The LORD's unfailing love and mercy still
> continue,
> Fresh as the morning, as sure as the sunrise.
> The LORD is all I have, and so in him I put my
> hope (Lam. 3:19–24 TEV).

I'm praying for your return of hope, dear Matthew.

My love,

A Son in Prison

Dear Mildred,

Even though we are acquaintances, all I really know about you or your son, Robert, is what I have read in the papers. Evidence, eyewitness testimony, and jury have judged him guilty as charged. I don't have any idea of what your other son, Bruce, is going through or how he feels, but I think, because I'm a parent and have a mother's heart, I can grasp just the edges of an idea as to how shattered your heart must be that you have lost one son to prison. It must be so hard to believe he's really there. And this tragic thing has really happened.

Since I have not walked in your shoes and do not know all the history or circumstances that surround each of you, all I can do is hold out my hand and give you grace.

I can give Robert grace instead of judgment. Understanding instead of condemnation. Love instead of ostracism.

I can also give you, dear Mildred, and your sons, Robert and Bruce, my promise of prayers for your hearts to heal and for you to feel hope once more. You have these two things—grace and prayers—for as long as you need them.

Grace and prayers,

An Argument

Darling,

When I read these words this morning, I thought, *That sounds like us!* I hope this helps.

> I said a lot of things. You said a lot more.
> I was hurt. You were angry and quite sore.
> What was I getting at? And what was it that
> you really meant?
> Who knows? I'm sorry, and I hope this note
> puts an end to the argument.

I love you,

Chronic Pain

Dearest Rosemarie,

Unless a person has experienced pain day after day after day like you have with TMJ [or some other chronic, debilitating illness], it is hard to understand why getting out of bed and facing another day of pain is so immensely difficult. Why go on? we ask. Why endure this savage beating of pain for one more day? Why indeed?

Dr. Viktor Frankl, a Holocaust survivor, wrote, ". . . To live is to suffer, to survive is to find meaning *in* the suffering."*

---

* Viktor Frankl, *Man's Search for Meaning* (Old Tappan: Washington Square Press, 1959), 11.

And while you and I might not feel or see any sense, much less *meaning*, in the ongoingness of our pain, it is painstakingly true that if we can hang on long enough, meaning comes!

I believe that much of our knowledge and wisdom, our most creative thoughts, and our greatest achievements are forged in the furnaces of our suffering. We can look back and say, "Ah, there was meaning in that after all!"

So, dear one, until you can begin to see meaning in your pain today, I'll see it for you. It will come about, dear one, and I believe *eventually* we'll see it happen together!

My love and prayers,

~

Finances

My dear Caroline,

Again and again I have rehashed and mulled over in my mind our phone conversation yesterday.

I've never stood or walked in your shoes, so I really don't know the extent of your painful despair. But to see your company, your home, and most of your material possessions sink out of sight into the black waters of bankruptcy must be unbelievably shocking to your heart, impossible to accept, and even more depressing to try and deal with!

So, besides sending you a package with treasured

things and some practical possessions for you to keep, I'm praying in this manner:

Lord, please give Caroline

enough *wealth* to support her needs,
enough *strength* to do battle with banks, IRS officials, lawyers, and so on so she will overcome this,
enough *grace* to endure and press on, and
enough *hope* to remove her anxiety attacks and her fears for the future.

We wait together, dear Caroline, to see what God and his people will do through all of this!

My love and prayers,

To My Friend

Dear Bob,

I write this just because I know you are hurting. And with me you don't have to pretend that it *doesn't* hurt, nor do you have to put up the front that you are handling things well. I know that nothing at this moment is hunky-dory.

Losing your job for *whatever* reason is, pure and simple, a very real form of rejection. I've never learned how to soothe the ache of rejection—either real or imagined—so

I don't have any great words of advice. Nor do I have any clichés like, "Oh, buck up . . . you'll be just fine."

But I want you to know two things:

1. I'm with you and I believe in your talents and unique gifts.
2. I would like to get together with you to think creatively about the next step or to do whatever you'd like to do.

The important thing is let's do it together. I trust that God's got a plan! And I know he can be trusted.

Love,

Multiple Crises

Dearest Debbie and Mark,

Shakespeare was right on target when he penned these lines about the abundance of pain and suffering:

> When sorrows come,
> They come not single spies,
> But in battalions (*Hamlet*).

By now, with the loss of your precious baby, Timothy, to sudden infant death syndrome, with Mark's dad's heart surgery, and now with the fire that destroyed your home and everything in it, you must be fairly certain the two of you are fighting several battalions and are completely losing the war.

I wouldn't fault you if your prayers right now are more in the form of a yell like, *Dear God! Will this ever stop? I've had enough!*

And as if to heat up the fires of your aching hearts, I overheard Mrs. Harrison tell you, "God is allowing all this pain so you'll learn a lesson from it and grow!" Her words must have smarted like vinegar as they poured over your raw wounds. I wanted to snap back at her, "Yeah, Debbie has grown so much in the past year, she's virtually a twelve-foot Jolly Green Giant and quite fed up with growing!"

Dear ones, try and keep this in mind: Our heavenly Father, who loves us beyond all measure, does not stick pins in us as if we were voodoo dolls, nor does he gleefully send us trials and losses just to test us or see if we'll grow. No. I don't think so.

However, it is true that suffering is a teacher, if an unwelcome one. Pain and suffering are a very real part of life. There will always be something or some experience that we cannot possibly find an answer to or understand right now . . . but I pray you'll take a measure of hope and peace of heart from these words of David: "Many are the afflictions of the righteous: but the LORD delivereth him out of them all" (Ps. 34:19 KJV).

Keep in mind that God *will* deliver you both. In the meantime hear the Lord say, "Fear not, for I am with you. Do not be dismayed. I am your God. I will strengthen you; I will help you; I will uphold you with my victorious right hand" (Isa. 41:10).

You are loved,

Multiple Crises

My dear Sharon,

The shattering events that have surrounded you these past two weeks are simply astounding. I pray that in time you will experience comfort and healing enough to see the long arm of God at work. Right now it must be terribly, terribly difficult for you to make any sense out of these multiple tragedies. *Overwhelmed* may be an understatement.

Of course, even if you *do* get a handle on some of this or find some rationale in all this confusion and pain, some well-meaning friend is just bound to slap you on the back and glibly spout Romans 8:28. You know, "All things work together for good . . ." As if you are the village idiot who's not familiar with that verse.

Personally I have seen the beauty of Romans 8:28, but I believe with all my heart after memorizing it in my childhood, that Romans 8:28 is not always a verse for right now—this moment. Often I feel it's a *hindsight* verse. It's an incredible illuminating truth that dawns on one sometimes *long after* the tragic events are over. It's like a truth that comes clear *later* when we turn around, look back, and say, "Oh, my, just look at how many things worked together for good." We can see clearly how God did this and that and even worked some miraculously wonderful things out, in spite of the circumstances of that dark, hideous time. But sometimes in the heat of battle, the good that God is bringing about is hidden from us by our blinding pain.

However, we both know how sweet it is, in the middle of the night, after the initial pain has subsided a bit, to hear the Savior as he whispers into your heart,

"Sharon, my child, I *am* making all these things work together for your good . . . trust me and my love."

I know you have a trusting relationship with the Lord and that if you listen closely, you'll hear his voice assuring you of Romans 8:28. So I'm praying that verse for you today. Just keep in mind: it's a *hindsight* verse.

My love,

Multiple Crises

My dear Beverly,

By now you're ready to give up on everything you ever believed in. You've had one tragedy pile on top of another. I heard the edge of desperate hysteria cutting through your voice on the phone. No wonder you asked, "When is all this going to stop? Will it *never* end?"

I have no idea why suffering comes in bunches — I only

know that it does. So please hang on. These sorrows now coming in wave after wave have got to end sometime. The tide has to go out at some point. So until it does, please know I'm with you, waiting. Waiting with you.

My love,

Relocation

Dearest Julie,

I weep with you as you are preparing to leave the town, church, and community that has been your home and a significant part of your life for so many years. I weep too that you will be going thousands of miles away to make your new home among strangers.

Just moving a couple of blocks down the street is never an easy task, but leaving family and friends is a searing pain unlike any other!

Today as I was crying and hurting with you over the necessary decision to relocate, I came across these words in Isaiah:

> I will make rivers flow on barren heights, and
> springs within the valleys.
> I will turn the desert into pools of water and
> the parched ground into springs (Isa. 41:18
> NIV).

Then I wondered, *Is this what our loving Lord is planning on doing for Julie as she begins her life again without those she loves and in a remote wilderness?* And I thought, "I can trust God with this." I know you'll be able to trust him, too.

My love,

Relocation

Dearest Jean Marie,

If I were you I'd probably crawl under the sheets of my bed, hibernate, and not come out until next Groundhog Day!

You are in the process of having to move, so you're dealing with one serious adjustment after another. And then there's the problem with changing attitudes—yours and others'.

I've no idea what I'd be like if my husband was transferred from his job here in Denver to Chicago! Nor what hoops would I jump through mentally and emotionally if I had to resign my job and look for a new one like you are going to have to do! Never mind the fact that you and I have just finally juggled all the working and personal schedules like carpools for the kids' schooling, choir practice, soccer, and Little League games! *Oi vey!*

I'll be over to help you with packing your dishes, etc., next Tuesday—if that's okay. But I'll be praying that, somewhere in all the bustling confusion of relocating, God will give you a few injections of joy!

Oh, boy! I can hear you scream from here, *"Joy???"*

Yes. Joy. At first I thought I'd ask God to give you happiness in this move, but I think joy is better. Much better. As I think of it, joy is an independent emotion. It's not tied to what's happening *around* us. It's welded to what's happening inside us. And believe me, I know, joy doesn't come and go or rise and fall like a kite on the end of a string.

Not at all, as you know—joy is a lovely, surprising gift from God. A gift that, in spite of all our moves and emotional quandaries, can spill out of us at the most unexpected times. Even when we're moving and relocating!

You can count on me next Tuesday, and you can count on my holding you up to God to be the recipient of his gift of joy for sporadic moments of your day!

My love, see you Tuesday,

Relocation

My dear Grandkids,

What can I say to help this move to Arizona make any sense or hurt less?

I know you're missing your best friends even now— *before* you've moved. And then there are all those other familiar and comfortable areas in your life. Like the kids at school, some teachers, church and soccer teams, and of course, your house, your room, and your dog Scruffy (who may not adjust to a new home any better than you). There must be a million memories.

So I'll just tell you for the umpteenth time that I love you and I'm convinced your parents love you—even when you are unable to understand them or their actions. And I feel in my heart that everything will, eventually, be all right. Maybe even better. Who knows?

But until *you* see things being right again . . . I'll be praying for a smooooth move and a dose of some healing medicine for your hurting hearts!

You are loved by your grandma! Me,

Abuse

My dearest Lisa,

Forgive me if I'm repeating some things I must have told you over the phone. (My memory doesn't always kick in the way it should!) But even if I said these things before, they bear repeating.

Because of the unspeakable and repulsive act of incest by your dad, you're bound to feel as if you're caught in the crossfire between anger, fear, irrational guilt, and other soul-searing emotions. But remember, *he* did this to *you*. He robbed you of your childhood, and his hideous act can still rob you of life even now as an adult. Please hear me—you cannot and must not take the blame or the responsibility for what he, as an adult, chose to do.

Moving on with your life, though it's what you long to do, is slow and arduous work. Far easier discussed than done. But I do understand your longing for the past to be put behind you and your desire to have peace of mind over all this.

Come to think of it, everyone craves peace, and we mustn't underestimate our fundamental need for it. Even babies need peace and often find it in a pacifier, in a blue blanket, or best of all, in their mother's or grandmother's arms.

So, darling, today I'm writing this so I can give you my homemade recipe for peace. It's for when you're feeling particularly uneasy, restless, and *un*peaceful, and it's called "The Five-Minute Treatment." It goes like this:

Recipe

Search out a quiet place like a closet, a
secluded porch, or a rocking chair in a seldom-
used room or wherever.
Sit down for five minutes.
Silently repeat these words to yourself.
Absorb their calming and healing meaning into
your soul. Memorize them and picture Jesus
saying them just to you—right where you sit in
your special quiet place. Hear his voice as
gently he whispers, "Peace I leave with you, my

peace I give unto you . . . let not your heart be troubled, neither let it be afraid" (John 14:27 KJV).

Repeat as necessary (which may be often).

I can't promise that this old-fashioned recipe will erase all the past, but I believe it will make a marked improvement in easing the painful strife that's going on within you.

In the meantime, I'll be praying for God's peace to enfold your whole being—from head to toe!

I send my love,

~

Painful Memories

My dearest Daughter,

You sounded wonderful on the phone today, and what welcome news you gave to me!

Yes, I did remember the last thing I said at the airport after my visit with you: that when I prayed for you I would be praying for the healing of your memories. And today, you said that that healing is happening. It's even happening in your dreams at night! Praise God!

Long after I hung up the phone (still thrilled by the unmistakable joy in your voice), it came to me that my mother (your grandma) prayed the same prayer for me over three *decades* ago! Vaguely I remember the problems

I was sharing with her, but vividly I recall her response. She leaned across the kitchen table, took my face in her hands, and gently said, "Oh dear, Joyce-honey, I'm going to pray for the healing of your memories." And for me, like for you, apparently, the moment became a giant step toward wellness. Again, praise God!

Do you know what? Maybe your grandma began a lovely memory and praying tradition, and someday you'll pray this prayer for my granddaughter and then she'll pray it to her daughter. What a wonderful measure of healing from the Lord to us mothers for our children. Hey, even this day is a great memory!

I'll keep on praying for the healing of memories in both of us.

Lovingly,
Mom

Abuse

My dear Lou Ann,

Ah! So everybody in your support group suffers from physical or sexual abuse, and no one seems to have endured your "type" of abuse?

Well, that may be true on the surface, dear one, but even if no one talks about the abuse of emotional neglect (your type and mine), I believe there are millions of people who would know and identify instantly with you and the pain you've experienced.

Abuse is not limited to a couple of categories or in its scope to wound and bring terrible pain into our lives. In fact, we are living proof that the *abuse of emotional neglect*, while not as hideous as physical or sexual abuse, is still a silent, stealthful, and steady killer of the human spirit.

But having said that, I know in my own life, when I acknowledged that the abuse of emotional neglect had *really* happened—that I didn't make it up—and I realized I couldn't change either the past or the person, I took a scary step. I decided to look inward to see if I could come up with a way not merely to survive but to have an acceptable (maybe even an *exceptional*) quality of life.

Next I prayed for myself. I asked God as his child to give me a large measure of courage. Courage to grow. Courage to risk failure. Courage to stop blaming anyone else for the ruts, pitfalls, and roadblocks in my life's progress. Courage to see myself, not through the eyes of the person who by neglect never saw me, but through God's eyes. And finally, courage to memorize Ephesians 1:4 from the Living Bible and the courage to live by those words.

God began slowly but graciously answering my prayers for courage. I felt that the strength had somehow evaporated out of the person who abused me by emotional neglect. He could no longer strangle me, as he *had lost his power* over me.

This is my prayer for you: "Dear God, give Lou Ann a generous portion of courage so she will grow into the gorgeous person you already see! And I thank you in advance for what you'll do for her."

My love and continued prayers!

~

Painful Memories

Dear one,

Yesterday I heard a friend say that we can't *change* the past but that we can try to *heal* the hurt from the past.

And I thought of how that's exactly what you are doing. In fact, you've taken great strides in the healing department. You've got a wonderful and godly therapist, a supportive spouse and family, and even though the perpetrator of the abuse continues to deny any part of it, you know the truth. You also know you can't change the past, so you're actively working on healing the terrible hurts. Good for you!

You don't handle or work on this throbbing pain alone. I'm standing with you, along with your loved ones, and together we will all see and rejoice in your progress toward wholeness.

Besides, God is faithful to us. He never sleeps. He hears our cries and in his time he makes *all things* beautiful. Even in all of this!

You are loved,

Rejection

My dear Michael,

Rejection. Oh, how I hate that word! It seems to me that rejection in any degree or form, real or imagined, delivers a torrential downpour of unbelievable pain flooding our souls, and we find ourselves believing we will surely drown in it.

My heart aches for the rejection you are now feeling—especially since I've had and felt similar pain.

Also, I'm quite aware that the pain of rejection is mild during the day compared with the way it chooses to hammer home its hardest blows in the dead of night.

I can remember sleeping in a glassed-in front porch up on the third floor of our apartment building when I was a little girl. And well I remember how terrified I was each night of the bears, lions, and tigers that jumped out at me from the wall above my bed.

Of course, as my mother repeatedly explained, the animals weren't real but merely shadows cast by the street light flickering through the branches of trees as the wind moved through them.

So, dear one, when the bears, lions, and tigers come out at night and sleeping becomes impossible, remember that the animals may be only shadows and that he who never slumbers or sleeps is guarding and protecting your soul against the ravages of rejection, and he is nourishing your soul with his changeless love.

He is, you know. . . . We can trust his judgments because he knows *all* the facts, even the ones about rejection—and still he loves us! Perhaps this is so true because God is not in the business of rejection. When we come to him, he's all about acceptance, and we can count on that.

I feel your hurt . . .

My love,

Thoughts of Suicide

My dear Josh,

From our conversation yesterday and from seeing the naked terror in your eyes, I know you are standing on the very brink of the bottomless chasm of lethal despair. I don't blame or fault you. The events of your life have been and are hideous.

But as I see you on that dangerous edge, I want to reach out to you, grab you, and tightly hold you so you can't fall into the abyss of suicide.

Since I've been on that same precipice, I've tried today to remember who or what saved my feet from slipping away and sharing the same fate as you are now contemplating.

For me, a large factor in not giving up and going over the edge was other people's words. Like the words from a dear friend who told me that if I *did* go, half of him would die with me. But he assured me that after I was gone he'd never *ever* speak unkindly of me. To this day I can't explain exactly why his words touched me so deeply. It seemed as if he were aware of the huge quantity of pain in my life that had driven me to this place of insanity and was assuring me he'd never forget me and that I'd always be loved in his memory of me, even if I took this drastic action to end my life.

The loving tones of his voice and message seemed to pull me back away from the danger zone, and I took my first shaky steps in a new direction. My friend, Clare, admonished, "If you feel yourself heading toward that cliff, *call me first!*"

Then, later, when the pain increased again and descended like a heavy burial shroud around me and I found myself heading toward the edge once more, there was one line from a letter my daughter wrote to me that stood out from all the others, "Mom, thank you for staying one more day . . ."

What I'm offering you, dear Josh, are those same words—Call me first. Please know that even though the struggle is enormous, I thank you for "staying one more day" . . . two more days and on and on.

You may feel utterly alone, dear one, but you are not. God, others, and I are here with you. We'll not abandon you, now or ever.

You are constantly in my heart and prayers.

Always.

Love,

Emotional Pain

Dear one,

    I can't begin to imagine your pain right now, but here's what I *do* know. For certain.

    As you go through the agony of this latest experience, I hold your hand in love, gently cradle you in my arms of prayer, and fervently wish for God to send you ministering angels *today*. Right now.

You are loved,

Special Words "Just Because"

My dear Reader,

Sometimes it is a very good thing to express ourselves on paper—*just because.*

"Just because" circumstances can vary—as you'll see in these notes—but I hope these examples will give your heart and mind a nudge toward writing to your kids, your family, your friends, and your other loved ones.

You don't need a special occasion like a birthday to tell someone you love him or her. You can express your love "just because."

Of course, these notes will take time to think through and write out, but that's what makes them precious to the ones who receive them.

Besides, it makes our own hearts feel good when we write a "just because" note.

Love,

Joyce

To My Children

Dearest Daughter and Son,

I write this note just because, once again, it's time for me to go back to the hospital for God only knows how long and for whatever is wrong now.

It worries me that one of these times I won't come back in any physical or mental shape to talk to you—or worse, I won't come back at all. So, since I want no unfinished business between us nor do I want you to misunderstand *exactly* what I think of you, I'll write.

From the first moment I laid eyes on you, my dear son, and two years later on you, my darling daughter, I was smitten with love for you. There was no need to wish or hope for the bonding process to begin because it already had. I think it must have happened early in my pregnancy, somewhere in between morning sickness and an intense appetite for beef tacos and strawberries.

Actually, seeing you each for the first time made my love for you a reality, and I've never, not even once, stopped or tried to curtail that love.

Look at you! You both are wonderful, wonderful specimens of great humanity. You're the best, and it must be in the genes as well, because greatness keeps showing up in the grandchildren you've given me, and I feel quite certain it will go on with succeeding generations.

So, basically, what I want to say is this—I love you. I love you. I love you.

Love,
Mother

To My Friend

My dear Paulette,

I wrote this note just because you are important to me and because you really are my friend.

It's been an eye-opener to me that, contrary to public opinion, I don't need dozens of friends for encouragement and support. One or two like you will do nicely, thank you!

I wrote the words below a long time ago. But when I came across them today, I realized (again) how blessed I am to have you as my "friend-with-history."

A friend is not afraid to look at me as I really
   am. And
what that friend sees inside me doesn't bring
   harsh
judgments,
instant critical outbursts
nor the desire to put an end to our
relationship.
A friend peeks and peers into the hidden depths
   of my soul
and instantly sees that I need some
lifting of my drooping spirits,
strengthening for my weakening resolve,
laughter about the situation or at myself,
and large amounts of loving *just because*
I'm me.

167

And I thought, *Yep! That sounds just like my friend Paulette!*

Love,

To My Friend

Dearest Lillian,

I write this note just because you phoned [wrote to or spoke to] me.

When I think about all the times you and I have eagerly called each other over the years, it's no wonder I smiled today when I read my own words in my journal. I must have been thinking of you when I wrote them.

> It was autumn.
> The golden leaves of life were falling,
> Paul was dying.
> He called for his *friends*.
> He asked that they come before winter.
> Amazing.
> The great and famous apostle,
> known and loved
> revered and respected
> by thousands, yet he
> knew he needed old and trusted friends.
> So he *called for them*.

And I thought, *Oh, I know how Paul felt . . . and they didn't even have phones back then—just the same needs.*

So call me. I'm as near as a phone.

My love,

To My Friend

Dearest Janet,

I write this note just because I miss you!

Today your name passed through my thoughts. I stopped what I was doing (the laundry), and wondered how it was going with you.

Did your son pass the broker's exam? How was your trip to Longboat Key, Florida? What hysterically funny/bad thing has your Irregular Person done lately? How's your heart? If you could have a gift (not limited by time or money) what would it be? You know, all those "friend-type" questions.

But just as soon as I wonder about how it's going with you I think, *Well, until I know for sure how she is today, I'll pray and ask God to send her what she needs . . . courage, strength, wisdom, joy, or whatever!*

Just know you are loved, prayed for, and missed today . . . by me.

Love,

To My Mother

Dearest Mother,

I write this note just because you have always listened to me, believed me, and been on my side.

Today when I read what one friend wrote to another, I thought of your constant stream of love toward me.

The friend said, "Thanks for being a quiet, graceful dove of love instead of a crummy old albatross . . . heaving its wings with discouragement."

You did that for me yesterday on the phone [in your letter or at dinner], and once more I'm rich because of you!

I love you,

Special Words about Breast Cancer

My dear Reader,

Four very important factors force my heart and mind to write the following notes.

- In this year alone, forty-six thousand women (and a few hundred men) will die of breast cancer.
- The chances of you personally getting breast cancer or of knowing someone (loved one, friend, or neighbor) stricken with this life-threatening disease are significantly high.
- Since medical science has yet to find a cure, all that doctors are able to do is to aggressively treat the symptoms and preach preventative health care and early detection. This situation makes for interesting, sometimes very complicated, interpersonal relationships among doctors, medical staff and

technicians, and patient—and all of these interactions tend to play a strategic part in the patient's wellness.

- Two years after discovering my own tumor (missed by a gynecologist and three mammograms), I am in a process of treatment that has included a mastectomy, breast reconstruction, chemotherapy, and every three months a medical checkup. So I'm two years into this and counting.

For me, the diagnosis of breast cancer has become, as it were, a giant, well-lit magnifying glass, enlarging and bringing sharply into focus who and what are important in my life.

So I write these notes to you all with tried-by-fire understanding, with tender, warm, affectionate compassion, and with some salient wisdom born out of not only my own journey but out of many of yours as well.

With hope,
Joyce

To My Daughter

My dearest Laurie-honey,

I know you're encompassed by one of the most painful emotional struggles of your life. I pray this note reaches through the rawness and touches your heart at the point of your most piercing pain.

My breast cancer has given birth to some powerful fears . . . in both of us. Your fears for me, my fears for you and my precious granddaughter Jennifer, for your aunt Marilyn and her four daughters, and our combined fears for all the women of our family. These terrors have swooped down like hungry vultures who wait and watch us in agitated silence, eager to pounce on our dying remains.

We are forced to admit that we shall from now on have to deal with the fact that our hopes, dreams, and plans as a mother or a daughter are being severely rearranged and perhaps forever altered. Cancer does that. We know neither of us will ever be the same again.

There is, however, a ray of hope on our horizons, honey. I believe that the bond of love that grew between my mother and me during her cancer diagnosis, surgery, chemotherapy, radiation, and untimely death at the age of fifty-seven will for us grow just as strong . . . or even stronger.

Even after all these years, I still treasure those wonderful memories with my mother after cancer struck. And I plan to give you, darling, as many or more of the same type of memories, for as long as I have one breath left in me.

So for now, dearest Laurie, try to keep this uppermost in your mind: This scary, quite appalling time, accompanied by the ever-present vultures, will come to an end even if one or both of us do not survive.

But here's the best part:

Our bond of love is stronger than the cancer.
Our bond of love is more resilient than the
   cancer.
Our bond of love will always outlast the cancer.
Our bond of love will continue *beyond* this
   earthly life!

Thanks be to God for those bonds of love, dear one! They will keep us sane and hopeful.

I love you,
Mom

To My Wife

My darling Wife,

I believe you when you say you cannot "imagine" yourself recovering completely from cancer. If I were in your shoes, especially now during chemotherapy treatments, probably I'd feel the same way.

The pressure from almost everyone—family, friends, doctors—for you to act like you don't feel this way is enormous. It's almost as if they believe that if you would only pretend that you don't feel what you really feel, then the pretense itself would make you well!

But what they don't understand is that pretending

won't change the cancer. Nor will it change your fear of what cancer might do to you. Pretending will only make people think you're "up" when really you're very down. This would give them relief, but it would only ignite the pent-up coals of fear within you.

I'm in a predicament. I *believe* your fears. They are the demons you are living with right now. But if I tell you that I accept those fears (and sometimes have them myself), it probably helps you to know that I believe you, but does it also fuel your fears? Or if I tell you that I think your recovery is possible, does that say I don't believe your fears or that you are just a negative person who would get better if you'd just get a positive attitude?

The ambiguity of the cancer makes knowing what to say to you so difficult. (If you *knew* the cancer was going to go one way or another, you could adjust; you're a tough lady [as they say after they've stuck you three times before finding the vein].) But one thing is *not* ambiguous: I love you with my whole being, and I will love you forever. I wish my own frailties were never a source of pain to you, but know that my heart is forever yours.

I love you forever and beyond,

SPECIAL WORDS ABOUT BREAST CANCER

To My Wife

My darling Wife,

I want you to know that *nothing*, absolutely nothing, changes the set-in-concrete fact that I love you!

Not your having cancer or chemotherapy;

Not your losing a breast or your hair;

Not your being too sick to be up and about and participating in life as you have always done;

Not your struggling with anger, fatigue, or depression.

Not one of these real and terrible things can wipe out or even alter my love for you.

So write it across your heart in large letters, "HE LOVES ME REGARDLESS OF THE EVENTS AND CIRCUMSTANCES OF MY LIFE—HE LOVES ME."

I meant my vows on our wedding day. You know, the ones that said, ". . . for better or worse, in sickness and in health, for richer or poorer . . ." I took those words, my darling, as a *forever vow*, and nothing will turn me away from them.

I adore you and will forever!

Your loving husband,

To My Grandma

Dear Grandma Joyce,

This is my thank-you card for the things you gave me when you were here. I'm really happy with my perm. I wish you were here to see it. It looks really good. You would like it.

How are you? Our family is doing great. I hope your cancer is coming along. [She meant my chemo treatments.] My mom was reading the newspaper about a kid who has cancer and lost his hair like you did. To make him not feel left out, his friends shaved their heads. I thought that was nice. We all love you. I'm going to bed. Bye!

> Love, your granddaughter [age 11],
> Jennifer

To My Grandma

Dear Grandma Joyce,

Goodnight, my *wonderful* grandma. I'm going to bed soon.

> Love, your *wonderful* granddaughter

Oh, I told my mom to give you these mental messages over the phone, but I'm writing them, too:

"I love you" and "You should keep on fighting."

Love, your wonderful granddaughter [age 11], Jennifer

To Our Grandma

Dear Grandma,

It's so good to have you out here in California to celebrate Christmas with us. I'm glad your chemo treatments are all over!

This present is for you from Ricky and me. We want it to represent our love and prayers that we send to you each and every day.

Since a phone call to you in Texas is so expensive, this ceramic praying angel (that looks so very much like you) will have to do. Please set her somewhere so you can see her every day. Okay? And think of us and our prayers.

We love you, Grandma, and miss you always.

Love,
April Joy and Ricky

To a Friend

Dearest Sheila,

You asked what is "sustaining" me these days, and I had to think a bit. Nausea and loss of energy make doing anything, including thinking, a very difficult task.

But I believe the things that mean the most to me, like the faces of my loved ones, books read to me by my cherisher, and music, to name a few, are sustaining me. I call them simple pleasures.

Of course, I can't sing or play the piano as I have always done, but I can *listen*. So this afternoon I played a tape and once again heard the beautiful song "In His Time" (by Diane Bell).

Funny thing about simple pleasures . . . I find them extremely healing and comforting. Just as today, for a few moments, when the lyrics and music washed over my soul, I was touched and sustained.

I pray you have joy today in "simple pleasures."

My love,

To a Friend

My dear Mrs. Miller,

You are an incredible teacher! Do you have any idea of the lessons you are teaching me through your cancer? I'm sure you're not ecstatic about your role in furthering my education, but let me tell you about one lesson.

It occurs to me, as I watch and study your present demeanor of "I'll not quit" and your ever-emerging strengths of spirit, that you are a living example of the elusive art of *practicing* patience.

I'm learning from you that healing *or* dying, contrary to our hopes, involves long increments of time. Patience has nothing to do with being instantaneous or moving at breakneck speed. Patience slowly dawdles or crawls along at a snail's pace.

As I watch you in pain, I understand only too well why patience is so hard to come by. But your persistent patience in life is teaching me that it is crucial if we are to learn to trust.

I choose, as you must have done at some point, to trust God about you and your cancer. Patiently I trust, knowing full well that nothing happens in the snap of a finger or sometimes not even in this lifetime.

I shall be patient. I shall hold on to patience, let go of my skittish and impatient fears about you, and trust in our heavenly Father to, *in his time*, make all things beautiful for you!

Thank you dear, dear teacher!

My love,

To a Friend

My dear Cynthia,

Just a quick note to tell you that since your biopsy yesterday showed invasive cancer, you'll probably be told the next step is surgery. So you're going to need a good surgeon.

Because of personal experiences, I suggest you look for a doctor who does breast cancer surgery *all the time*. Ask the doctor, the doctor's nurse, or someone at the hospital where the doctor practices *how many* breast surgeries he or she does in a year. You want a doctor with as much experience as you can get. Some doctors (and other people) think it's demeaning to ask about how many of these surgeries doctors do per year—but I think it may be life-savingly important, both at the time of surgery and for your recovery later.

Also, don't be afraid to get several opinions. If you were hiring a person to work for you, you'd require references. For your health and peace of mind, obtaining several opinions is like getting a long list of references whereby you'll be better informed, better able to understand, and better— much better—at making appropriate choices for the most healing treatment options for yourself.

I know this is all new and quite scary, but for those of us who have gone through it in the past, our hindsight is excellent.

I'm with you, and if you want, I can highly and confidently recommend my oncologist and my surgeons.

You are loved,

To a Friend

My dearest Susan,

I know *exactly* what you mean!

Waiting, in general, for *anything* or for anybody is difficult at best, but waiting for medical test results takes the prize in nerve-wracking and stress-producing predicaments.

No wonder you are terribly upset. To be held in a state of suspended animation completely chafes the mind; emotionally, it's akin to being put on hold after you've just dialed 911.

And have you noticed that waiting for test results is not the only time we're going to wait?

We wait at the oncologist office for the doctor.

We wait for the nurse to find and puncture a vein for a simple blood test. Then, when the blood is finally drawn we wait for that signal, that look, that lack of eye contact, or those two reassuring words, "Looks normal."

We wait when our breasts are mashed down between the cold plates of the mammogram machine.

We wait for the phone call that we hope will announce, "Your mammogram is normal." Or the call that we dread the most, "The doctor would like you to come in so he can talk with you."

We wait after the biopsy, after surgery, and after we go home.

We wait if there's an emergency development while

some loved one tries to get a doctor or nurse to talk to you or to phone you back to tell you what to do.

What am I trying to say to you, dear Susan?

It's simply this: In all of life it seems that we are always in God's waiting room—waiting, waiting, and waiting for one reason or another. That's the bad news.

The good news is that I'm not going to let you wait alone. I'll be waiting *with* you, either in person or in spirit. And I'll wait with you for as long as it takes because it's easier to wait *together!* And best of all, God is with us as we wait.

My heart's with you.

Love,

~

Follow-Up to a Friend

Dearest Susan,

Hello. It's me again. Telling you I'm still waiting *with* you.

It seems to me that waiting, especially for test results, is a little like dying. It takes forever to get there, yet it's always on our heart's doorstep.

Just keep remembering what I said: We wait together!

My love,

To My Friend

Dearest sweet Martha,

At church yesterday, Pastor made the grim announcement that your cancer has spread to your lungs and that you've been hospitalized again.

Your name and lovely face have been in my mind's eye all day. The last time I saw you at church was just a couple of months ago at your husband's funeral. My heart asks how can you take any more pain and suffering?

Pastor said that when he visited you on Saturday, there was a beautiful glow about you, even though cancer is ravishing your body. I thought, *No big surprise there. This woman has walked in Winter's Valley before.* I can still picture you at Howard's funeral. Head up, tears streaming down your face. But your quiet courage and calm, dignified spirit reached out and touched all of us who sat there and watched. None of us will ever forget the moment.

Wednesday A.M.

I was still thinking of you today when I happened to read David's words in Psalm 17:15: "But as for me, my contentment is not in wealth but in seeing you and knowing all is well between us. And when I awake in heaven, I will be fully satisfied, for I will see you face to face."

Is that your secret, Martha? Are you filled with this deep, settled peace because God did for you what he did for David? I think so. Maybe you're on to something here! A lesson I can learn . . . thank you!

My love,

To a Friend

Dearest Esther,

Oh, no! It's back! Judy called me about you, and as I understand, it's not the return of breast cancer but two *new kinds*. Lung and bone . . .

This all seems so wrong and so unfair. You're too young, too special—a thousand other reasons burst inside my head. Of course, you already know all this, but I wonder: If *I'm* having such a hard time accepting this awful news about you, what must you and your loved ones be going through? Dear God!

I guess we should be extremely grateful for the three years you've had since your mastectomy, and yes, we are. But I have to confess that this spine-chilling turn of events has left me profoundly perturbed and has filled me with an outrageous quantity of sadness.

All I can say about today is that my heart and prayers are with you. Actually the name *Esther* is at the top—the very top—of my prayer list.

And all I can say about tomorrow is that I'll be over to your house with a big pot of my Hungarian goulash. I've decided that, at least for now, stew made with love is the very best way for me to deal with these new cancers and perhaps the very best way for you to have a small measure of comfort and love from me.

Enjoy, dear one!

Love,

To a Friend

Dearest Kimberly,

I had to smile. Your note asked me how I was handling breast cancer and all the horror that goes with it. For a second there, my mind saw an instant replay about losing my hair after my first chemo treatment. It took about four days for me to go scruffy-looking bald, and then my eyebrows and eyelashes gave up and gently fluttered to the floor.

In my mind's ear, I could hear my mother admonish: "Make the best of every situation." So I did. I got extremely creative with scarfs, hats, and sunglasses, but as anyone who's gone through chemo knows, it's a devastating and humiliating ordeal—bar none! And I know I didn't have much of a sense of humor regarding my hair loss. However, what was mildly funny and certainly puzzling was that all during those hairless months I still had to shave my legs. Go figure.

So, Kimberly, this is where we begin in coping and dealing with cancer: We make the best of it all, and we try to find some large chunks or tiny fragments of humor wherever and whenever we can.

Unfortunately coping with cancer is not a class or a course we can go take, learn from, and then pass a test to prove we've mastered the subject. Coping is like a slow intaking of information from other cancer patients, from medical authorities, and from people, books, TV, movies and other media forms.

For me, some of the most helpful and sound advice was from cancer survivor, Kathy La Tours, in her book *The Breast Cancer Companion* (William Morrow and Company, Inc., 1993). On a daily basis I have taken to heart her suggestions to (1) sort out my feelings, (2) keep hope alive, and (3) prepare for the inevitable.

On the medical side, I have received the most comprehensive view about dealing with breast cancer and understanding it better from *Dr. Susan Love's Breast Book* (Addison-Wesley, 1990).

I also have found the Living Bible's paraphrase of these words from Proverbs 16:1 quite valuable, and I keep them written on my desk blotter: "We can make our plans, but the final outcome is in God's hands."

However, all these wise bits of knowledge have sunk into my mind and heart like a free-floating feather—very slowly!

So be patient with yourself, dear Kimberly . . . I'm keeping you in my prayers.

My love,

To a Friend

My dearest Marion,

It's amazing, isn't it? We women with cancer seem to be surrounded by people who glibly say, "Hey, don't sweat this because medical science has come a long way!" Or they give us a personal example with, "My goodness, my grandma had breast cancer twenty years ago and she's still here with us and in her eighties!"

When I'm patted on the back and hear others express this attitude, I know several things. It's for sure *they* don't have cancer! It's also true that generally they are simply insensitive—not mean or cruel, just insensitive and oblivious to our struggle. But I have to admit that when I hear this kind of trivia, even from well-meaning people, the "spirit of slap" tends to rise quickly within me.

Yes, it's true that medical science has taken some giant strides lately, and the level of our awareness and self-examinations has certainly escalated; still, no one has found a cure, nor can anyone tell us how we get cancer in the first place. This mystery constantly brings us both to that unspoken, scary question lying in the viscera of our souls: "Will I be one of the forty-six thousand women who dies of breast cancer *this* year? next year? five years from now?"

I guess, dear Marion, that live or die, we both will have to trust our own judgment and common sense about cancer. We'll have to take under advisement the counsel of the medical community and continue to believe that God will lovingly provide exactly the right information as to what's best for us.

In the meantime, when insensitive remarks are made, watch out for that spirit of slap! This is no time for us to squander precious energy slapping others. On the other hand . . .

My love,

To a Friend

Honey,

With your cancer, or with any life-threatening illness, you must not rely solely on medical facts and data but look to your own heart for answers as well.

Keep in mind that you are the very first to know and hear what your body is trying to tell you. And believe me, your body will give and do far more than merely hint at what's going on.

You asked for my advice especially for you as a woman. Here it is:

- *Listen*. To your doctor, your body, your heart, and the still, small voice of the Lord.
- *Read*. Gather pertinent information from the widest variety of sources—from the Bible, to *Dr. Susan Love's Breast Book* (Addison-Wesley Publishing Co., Inc., 1990), and everything else in between.

SPECIAL WORDS ABOUT BREAST CANCER

- *Question.* Ask your doctor about *anything* that troubles you concerning your health. Request copies of test results and your medical records. And should your doctor respond to you as if you don't have a brain in your head or you're being "unreasonable" and a "bad" patient because you ask, leave! Find a doctor who listens *and* answers. (They're out there, I know, because I finally found one!)

- *Develop* this mentality: This is my body and my cancer. I have the right to have my questions answered and my fears and anxieties reasonably explained. And I need to remind myself that my medical records are just that: *my* medical records.

- *Write.* Keep a simple, dated journal. Don't edit it or worry about grammar or who might read it. This record is for your eyes only, a mirror of your emotions. I predict it will be therapeutically healing for your soul, time after time.

- *Remember.* You have friends like me who care.

My love,

To a Friend

Dearest Charlotte,

Before this is over, you are going to get weary, like most of us, of hearing the medical advisers tell you that you are "in charge of choices." And that "the decision is up to you." Well, that's not 100 percent accurate.

When I finished chemo treatments, I was told by my oncologist that I had "a window of three weeks to decide on taking radiation," but that he felt I definitely *should* go ahead with it. He implied that *his* decision was the right one.

During that "window of three weeks," I read everything about radiation for left breast surgery, got a second and third opinion, and changed to an oncologist who gave me even more medical data to read and evaluate. After studying my pathology reports, the new doctor did *not* recommend radiation for me.

After evaluating everything from doctors and on my own, I know the decision *not* to go with radiation was the very best decision for *me*.

That's the key to your treatment—what is the best choice for *you*? Go with your head *and* your heart so you will be sure it is your choice.

Don't give up. . . . Carry on!

Love,

To a Friend

Dearest Barbara,

As you begin your chemo treatments, take this short Scripture with you. It comforted me during chemo, and perhaps it will soothe your heart as well.

. . . as I was with Moses, so I will be with thee (Josh. 3:7 KJV).

See, in your mind's eye, the Lord going with you and whoever accompanies you (your husband or friend) each time you go to the doctor's office, lab, or hospital.

We can trust in God, for he will keep his word. He will be with you!

My heart goes with you, too.

My love and prayers,

My dear Reader,

As you may already know, my mother died of breast cancer in 1966.

On the following page are a few excerpts from her last note to me before she was admitted to the hospital. Mother was told she would be home in a couple of days, because they were just going to drain her lungs.

She took the doctors at their word, but just in case something went wrong, she wrote this letter so I'd know of her love for my brother, my sister, and me.

I cherish her last line, especially because she remained at the hospital and died there seven weeks later.

Sometimes our handwritten notes can say good-bye in a most eloquent way. This note from my mother helped me with that elusive thing called closure. And to this day I repeat her loving admonition to "Keep faith with God, regardless and always." And I am warmly comforted.

Love,

Joyce

SPECIAL WORDS ABOUT BREAST CANCER

To My Children

My dearest Children,

I thank God for such dear grown children and for your love and concern for your mother.

Of course I'm so pleased that the chickenpox has finally gone from my precious grandchildren and that the new job is going great for my Son-in-Love.

Next week three ladies from the church are coming over to clean my house for me. They'll clean windows, polish the furniture, vacuum, etc. Goodness knows the place needs it!

I must close. It's almost noon, and I have to go back to the hospital.

So much love and prayers for you, my dear children.

Keep faith with God, regardless and always.

Lovingly yours,
Mother

Special Words
Never Mailed

~

My dear Reader,

No, I'm not out of my mind.

There really is a great deal of therapeutic venting, releasing, and healing that takes place when we write notes without the enormous emotional pressure of actually mailing them. Writing a never mailed note also eliminates the agonizing wait for the recipient's response, or lack thereof.

Notes to family members dead or alive, notes to former friends, husbands, or wives, even notes to God and loved ones in heaven (which obviously *can't* be mailed) provide an excellent method of sorting through and venting away some of our most crippling thoughts. We can write without the threat of a reply, and in doing so we can become more objective in our thoughts, and we can better sort out and analyze our relationship with the person we're writing to.

In fact, something else you might want to consider in your never mailed letter is to present it to the Lord *as you write it.*

Remember King Hezekiah? No? That's all right; I didn't either until a friend reminded me. The king *received* a letter, and after he read it, he went up to the temple and "spread it before the LORD." Then he prayed and poured his heart out to God (Isa. 37:14 KJV). I think it's comforting to know that even when we are composing or receiving a never mailed letter we can bring it to the Lord—knowing he accepts our feelings as they are. Also when we write out our feelings, perhaps it helps us to open our hearts more to God as it seemed to do with King Hezekiah.

What I love best about writing a note never to be mailed is that as I articulate my anxieties on paper, they seem to lose some of their emotional steam. Fears are made smaller; they are no longer lurking about my soul with such power. And anger is vented, bringing a measure of relief.

Another friend of mine suggested writing two letters. One letter that gets out all the bottled up hostilities within us is never mailed. But a second letter, written in a much calmer frame of mind, *is* mailed. The choice is up to you.

But whichever way or method you choose, I encourage you to write with no-holds-barred honesty. Write without a need to cover up for yourself or others. Write with an open heart and an eye toward what is true and what is false in your words. In the case of writing to an abuser or to the perpetrator of a crime, you might want to enlist the help of a counselor or therapist before you write.

But by all means, write. And stay away from stamps and post offices!

Love,

Joyce

Hey, Harvey,

~~Killed anyone lately with your pious but snide and deadly remarks?~~

Destroyed some person's career with your innuendos of doubt about his or her skills or character?

Cut off any long-time friends because they no longer suit your purpose or feather your nest?

No?

How refreshing. What did it take to make you change your ways? Never mind answering—I just realized it doesn't matter!

Sincerely,

Dear God,

Thank you for giving me a 24-carat-gold cherisher!

Could you please arrange to tell him (again) in his heart of hearts how much I love him and that he's the very best? Somehow when I tell him that I love him, it doesn't sink in.

However, I think when special words and compliments come from someone else—like you, God—they are more easily accepted and have more validity. Oh, I do love him so!

I love you, too,

Dear God,

One of your choicest servants, Phillip Brooks, a minister who preached during Abraham Lincoln's time, wrote (as you already know) these powerful words:

Pray the largest prayers.

Pray not for crutches but for wings!

And, Lord, I'm doing just that. But oh, my, right now it's terribly difficult. I'm at an impossible intersection— again. It's decision time—again. Which route shall I take? The road on the left leads directly into a murky cesspool twenty feet deep. And on the right? A sheer cliff drops off and disappears into the rocks on the shoreline below. With either way I choose, I'm a goner.

So, dear heavenly Father, here it is—my largest prayer, not my longest—but it is simply, *Jesus, intervene. Please.*

Your daughter,

Dear God,

I'm really struggling here.

I feel like there's a multitude of voices shouting out to me, all agreeing I must do more and more praising in my prayer life. It's the "theology of praise" to some and is also their big catch-all trash basket. The simple answer to life's every problem. The voices assault me and say it's my fault if my life is hurriedly being flushed down the toilet. Why is it my fault? Because I'm not giving a "victorious testimony" full of praise to you at the Wednesday night prayer meeting or to Mrs. Wilson when I run into her at the grocery store.

So I'm struggling.

Actually I have no problem with praising you. I love you, dear Lord! My life has been, and still is, in your loving hands. And you know that I'm not so blinded by the pain of brokenness that I cannot see the evidence of your love as I look about my home or see your face in the faces of my loved ones. You've been generous with your precious gifts to me, and I am grateful. But still I struggle with the day-to-day grinding and polishing process called life.

Here are my fears, my failures, my frustrations. See? They are not exactly pinnacles of praise to you; in fact, they are just the reverse. What's that you say? Okay, I will praise you—with my intellect, my emotions, and my spirit. But you know, the space between my fear feelings and my ability to praise you right now looks like a vast, unbridgeable canyon.

I'm asking (no, pleading—a step up from begging) that you strengthen the weak tissues of my feelings. Give me courage to reach out to touch what I know is truth. And one more thing: As I accept the fact that struggling is a very normal process, please provide elasticity to my heart so that I don't become rigid or (worse) paralyzed with daily fears, doubts, and disappointments.

Today and for all my tomorrows, help me continue on track and, at the same time, lie back in your everlasting arms. (What a dichotomy here!) Even in my struggle I can see your long arms reaching out to me, and I'm filled with awe and praise. Really. I am.

I do so love you, dear God, and believe that you love me whether I'm struggling or not. For today, that's more than enough.

I'll try to remember your awesome goodness to me, especially when I see a new struggle peeking around the corners of my mind. I *will* praise and trust you. As David said, "This is the day which the LORD hath made; we will rejoice and be glad in it" (Ps. 118:24 KJV)!

Hey, look at me—I'm rejoicing!

Your child,

Dear Linda,

It's been many years since our friendship and close relationship ended. Seeing you at dinner the other night made me examine and ask myself why my heart hurt so much. I guess I'd hoped we'd be "lifelong" friends, not just friends for a brief passage of time.

I don't intend to pin you on the mat because of the past nor do I want to cause you any unpleasantness, but I need some kind of closure. And I think it would help me if I could, by writing this note, feel some healing in my old wounds and still-painful scars.

First, I'll always love you as my friend and roommate in college, and I don't for one second regret having you as my maid of honor in my wedding. Nor can I ever forget all the silly and fun times we had together, especially at the restaurant just off campus. Those experiences still warm my heart and make me smile.

But your abrupt departure out of my life, without explanations, and your immediate friendship with my sister was and still is a small but open wound within me.

After seeing and briefly talking with you the other night, and after thinking and praying about this, it occurred to me that maybe God places two people together in a friendship just for that *specific time.* He gives us brief but special friendships for our development, our education, or our emotional needs of the moment. (The words from Mordecai to his niece Queen Esther come to mind: ". . . for such a time as this" [Esther 4:14 KJV]).

If this is true, then even though it's a bit painful to see you at various places and family events, I can be thankful to the Lord that once, for a time, we were friends.

Please know that you're in my heart of hearts, and I'll always hope and wish the very best for you.

With memories,

SPECIAL WORDS NEVER MAILED

Dear Dad,

It's absolutely mind-boggling to think that you, with a straight face, could look me in the eye and piously say, "I stood before Jesus, and I don't believe the incident ever happened."

Excuse me, Dad, it wasn't an *incident* that happened—it was *incest*.

One of the best things about Jesus is that he knows *all* the facts. He even knows all the dirty details of the sexual molestation you perpetrated on me when I was a little girl. And incidentally, I seriously doubt that Jesus would have described your abuse as "an incident."

However, *because* and *in spite of* those repulsive acts of yours, I've been forced to become an adult at an early age, and later to seek godly professional help. So you see, Dad, even though you are calling me a liar, good will come out of the bad days of my childhood. God will see to it.

I am well on my way to healing now, even though you did rob me of so many things. And whether you confess or admit your guilt in the things you did is not the issue here. I *know* you did it. What I'm writing about is to tell you that you no longer control me—and you never will again in any way. You can deny the truth all you want, refuse to take responsibility for your acts—whatever. You can write or not write, call or not call. Actually, I do care how you feel, but I will not let that control me. And incidentally, I'm not impressed with the role you are now playing as "Mr. Good Christian."

I don't know how long you'll live or what eventually

will take your life. But I suspect you'll die from exhaustion, because secrets are very heavy burdens. And they are weighty whether we acknowledge them or not.

'Bye for now,
Your daughter

My dearest Mother,

Why is it that even after almost thirty years, I still miss your face, still long for your gentle touch, still want to hear your voice (especially in prayer), still wish we could talk on the phone like we did, shop in our favorite stores, or communicate with each other for hours and never finish? Why is this?

Oh, I know I'll see you one day in heaven, and it will be incredibly wonderful! But today, on Mother's Day, I wish you were here—or that I were there.

Your death taught me many things, and you left me with a vast inheritance of wisdom and love . . . but I still miss you.

So happy Mother's Day, dear Mother. By the way, do they celebrate Mother's Day in heaven? I don't know, but I'll tell you this: When I get there, you and I are going to have one great party, with or without Mother's Day.

I love you, Mother,

Special Words to Neighbors

My dear Reader,

It may sound rather silly to write a note to someone who lives next door or just a few blocks away. But with hectic family schedules, time pressures, and stressful incidents in our lives every day, maybe writing a note isn't such a bad idea.

Writing an occasional note to the people who live nearby makes perfect sense (at least to me), because it's another way of keeping the channels of communication open.

Let's face it: No matter how busy or how uninvolved we are with the daily business of being alive, writing a note may well nurture and touch another's soul at the right moment. And while we may be loath to admit it, we all suffer from some degree of urban loneliness.

I've only given you a few examples here—just enough

to encourage you to write. Notes can be slipped under our neighbors' door, delivered by a child, placed in their mailbox, or stuck under their windshield wiper. I believe that not only during the length of time it takes our neighbors to read the note but for some time afterward, they will be warmed and grateful for these short missives from us. Our neighbors are important people—and it's nice to tell them so.

Love,

Joyce

Dear Caroline and Fred,

Just a note to say thank you for being such wonderful neighbors.

Even though we don't see each other very often, still we don't want to take you for granted.

We admire your pride of ownership that keeps your yard so beautiful. (I especially love the bright-pink geraniums that are blooming right now.) We enjoy the friendly sounds of your voices calling out greetings to us. And we are grateful for your watchful eyes when we are out of town.

Simply put, we are blessed to be the people living next door to you!

Our thanks,

Hello dear Walter,

You know I love your big Irish setter, Rusty, but he's been tramping through our newly planted beds of pansies. Those pansies were costly, and because we're over the hill in age, it took us a long time to plant them. (The old grey mare . . . ain't what she used to be.)

Today I took matters into my own hands after I caught Rusty in the act again. I told him to cut it out and stop running and ruining those flower beds. He took it quite well. I think he even smiled.

But he said you told him it was okay!

Did you really say that?

Your loving next-door neighbor,

Dear Mr. Geiger,

You and your wife have just got to be *the* most kind and patient neighbors in the whole world.

When our fifteen-year-old Danny backed our car into your stone wall a week ago (ruining not only the wall but your beautiful garden behind it), you easily could have angrily exploded and started a petition to get us moved out of the neighborhood.

But did you do that? No siree! You just calmly surveyed the damage, took it in your stride, and quietly agreed to our getting the wall fixed as quickly as possible. And best of all, it was as if you absolutely refused to let all that destruction erode or dampen our friendship as neighbors.

I also noticed you graciously accepted Danny's lengthy apology and resisted the urge to tear his learner's permit into tiny pieces.

Thank you! You two really are the best neighbors in the whole world.

Oh, by the way, I know that from now on Danny will be a *whole* lot more careful when he's backing up! He is also planning on doing twenty-five hours of community service—if you'll let him—to help you restore your garden.

We are grateful to be your neighbors,

Dear, dear neighbors,

You all have been so kind and caring during our recent family tragedy. We hardly know where to begin in thanking you for all the countless expressions of support you have blessed and given us.

John and I decided that one way we could show our gratitude was to have a backyard barbecue and pool time together for you and your kids. So sometime within the next four weeks, I'll be phoning you to set a date. But in the meantime, we didn't want another day to pass without you knowing how special you are to us.

We are deeply touched and thankful for your loving support and friendship.

Your grateful neighbors,

SPECIAL WORDS

Special Words of Apology

My dear Reader,

Just as I know that without the glorious ingredient called *hope* in our souls we give up and slowly die, I know also that without the presence of apologies and forgiveness in our souls, the *quality* of life suffers greatly, while the vines of bitterness are fertilized and grow strong.

Apologies are difficult enough because we become vulnerable for what we actually said or did. Apologies are doubly hard and humiliating because, the moment we admit our fault or error, we can be accused of even more than we did!

No one ever said that apologizing—saying "I'm sorry" or asking "Will you forgive me?"—is an easy thing to do, but I think that writing a note of apology is just a tad easier than going through the trauma of a face-to-face encounter. And oh, yes, a friend of mine suggested that if you *do* have a face-to-face encounter with someone, and sincere apologies are given or exchanged, here's a great follow-up. It is a heartwarming gesture of grace to send a note to him or her *the next day*. It can affirm one's feelings and at the same time confirm one's spoken responses.

Yet any apology, written or spoken, requires that our pride step aside, our egos lie down, and we accept the risk, by all accounts, that we make ourselves vulnerable targets. All this awareness goes into making apologies significantly scary.

We may think, *Whoa! What if my words are not taken seriously? What if he or she uses them against me at a later time? What if I say "I'm sorry," and he or she responds, "Well, you should be!"? Or what if absolutely nothing happens—no healing, no opportunity to change my behavior, no chance for reconciliation or restitution? Or what if someone dies before I can apologize, and I'm left with unfinished business and no window of time for closure? In fact, why apologize at all?*

I've asked myself these same questions, but I've come to believe that a great deal of mental and emotional healing can take place during an apology. I believe, too, that apologizing is worth the risk of humiliation or rejection. Perhaps this is why the ninth step of AA's twelve-step program, which is about one making *amends* with another, is so powerful in bringing wholeness and well-being to hurting souls.

Rarely is it too late for apologies. I was in my thirties when my mother, just a few days away from her death, asked my forgiveness for a decision she had made when I was in my teens. The moment is one of my most cherished memories. I find it quite remarkable when a parent apologizes to a child or vice versa. "I'm sorry. Will you forgive me?" nurtures and bonds all at once.

I do have a few words of caution for notes of apologies, however:

Apologies should not be lumped into one-size-fits-all categories. Those broad, expansive, or vaguely written apologies that state, "*If* I've ever done anything in my entire lifetime to hurt you, please forgive me," hardly cut the mustard. In fact, an unspecific apology, such as, "Can you find it in your heart to forgive me for whatever you believe I did to hurt you?" only stirs up more anxiety; the person apologizing is taking no responsibility for what he or she did—and is laying on a burden of guilt in the process. A friend of mine calls this type of wording an Attorney's Apology: "I confess to nothing, but if I'm guilty of anything, forgive me and please be lenient on me."

So we need to keep our wording specific. We also need to take responsibility for our part in the matter.

The aim of our apology should be reconciliation, which can so beautifully come from those special, healing words "I'm sorry. Will you forgive me?"

Love,
Joyce

SPECIAL WORDS OF APOLOGY

My dear Jeff,

Even though our friendship is a hundred-plus years old (well, okay, I'm only kidding), you have every right in the whole world to walk away and never speak to me again!

Mentally, I've gone over our last conversation, and I realize (I can't believe I did this!) my small and stupid remarks about your relationship with Jenny were definitely inappropriate on my part and certainly unsolicited on your part.

Actually, I stepped way beyond the parameters of our friendship. I was completely wrong to speak so critically of Jenny, especially since I don't have all the facts—nor did I consider, even for a moment, your feelings in all of this.

I know my words offended and hurt you (not to mention what they did to Jenny), and they ended up putting a rather formidable wedge between us.

I am so sorry for the hurt I caused you.

You are a wonderful friend, and I don't want anything to interfere with our friendship.

Please forgive me.

Love,

My dearest Son,

My ability to jump straight to the wrong conclusion about you ranks right up there with my uncanny ability to assume that I know what you did, or worse, what you are thinking. (Oh, you've noticed.)

Well, I saw myself this morning in the bathroom mirror (not a pretty sight) and thought of how I bungled things yesterday between us.

Honey, I am sorry. Please forgive me.

Next time we are in a difficult situation, I will try to keep my mouth shut until I've heard your side. And I'm getting rid of my Nike running shoes to cut down on my ability to jump to conclusions about you.

You are not just loved by me but cherished as well.

Love,
Mom

~

Dear Mom,

I know I apologized to you before I went to bed last night, but it just hit me that I need to write out an apology for something else.

When we had our little fight in the kitchen, were in the heat of the battle, and I told you that you . . . well, you know what I said . . . I just realized that Dad and Grandma were sitting in the den. They overheard the whole thing.

So I am sorry, not only for what I said, but for embarrassing you in front of Dad and Grandma.

I love you. You're cool, Mom!

Your son,

Dear Rene,

Last Tuesday I had lunch with three women we both know. Your name came up, and one thing led to another. Suddenly I found myself bad-mouthing you about your decision to file for legal separation from Bill. I was proud that "I'd never do *that!*" And I was almost gleeful as we gossiped about what you and Bill are going through. Unfortunately no one, least of all me, suggested that we love you through this terrible time.

Earlier today I called the friends who were at the luncheon and told each of them that I was wrong in judging you and in compounding the problem by gossiping about you. I said I was sorry for my behavior, and I do not intend to do anything like that again! Ever!

Now I ask your forgiveness. I'm very sorry I said those things, and I'm deeply ashamed of myself. Please forgive me.

I believe I've learned a valuable lesson from this. I hope I can earn your trust and respect again so we can be friends.

Warmly and truly sorry,

Dear MaryAnn,

I'll make this short and sweet . . .

I confess that I really damaged the bridge of our friendship by my words last Monday night. I had no right *whatsoever* to be critical of the way you and Roger are handling Debbie's problems. I am so sorry.

Please forgive me.

Could we start the rebuilding as soon as possible?

Your friend,

Special Words at Bedtime

My dear Reader,

I'm not sure exactly when I got the idea to leave notes on my son's and daughter's pillows at night. But it seems to me that I started leaving notes from the time my children were nine and eleven years old and continued the practice until they were grown—off to college, moved, married, or whatever came first.

The notes were most often a short "'Atta-boy" pat on the back or a warmly written verbal hug. And when my kids became teenagers, notes were a great way to address and make some headway on our disagreements *without* the heat of face-to-face combat.

What I didn't count on was the bonus of finding notes on *my* pillow. Notes like "Mom, please fix these pants for me. Your son, Rick." And a note from my daughter Laurie that puzzled me as much as when I received it as it does now: "Dear Mom, Don't take my pillow away. It's holding my hair in place." I saved all notes, counted them as missives of love, and gave them back to my kids when they celebrated their fortieth birthdays. What memories those notes conjure up!

I encourage you to try this at your house; write notes to the loved ones closest to you. I know for a fact that our on-and-off ritual of leaving bedtime notes enhanced our lives and made us all feel richer in our hearts.

Talk about bonding!

Love,
Joyce

Dear Kevin,

I was so proud of you today, even though you guys lost the soccer game. Your dad and I thought you tried your best, and really trying's pretty important.

And when you got hit by that big kid and went down so hard, I held my breath. But you got up—no fuss, no muss, no problem—and went on. Good for you! (Judy held me back so I wouldn't run out on the field and embarrass you!)

I love you, honey.

Mom

P.S. I'd be proud of you even if you *didn't* play soccer . . . so there!

My dear Lisa,

I know that teenagers don't think their parents *ever* listen to them, and maybe this afternoon it really felt that way to you . . . but I did listen, and I did hear you.

Let's see if I've got this right. You want to go to Debbie's house on Friday and stay overnight. There's no school on Saturday, so why did I say no?

I think you know, but let me write it out for you. Debbie's parents are out of town for the entire weekend, and no adult will be there. Does it make any sense to you that I said no?

Yes, you are fifteen, old enough to take care of yourself, but we don't live in a perfect world, honey. If we did, I'd have no fears about your safety and no doubts about your going and having a blast. I'd even help you pack your stuff and send brownies with you.

You also asked (screamed), "Don't you trust me, Mom?" And my answer is still, "Yes, Lisa, I trust *you* — it's all those unknown factors and unexpected people in this imperfect world that I don't care to rely on or trust."

It's like your learner's permit. I know *you* are a careful driver — very safety conscious. I'm proud of the way you drive. I trust your driving skills, your judgment, and your quick reflexes. But what about *other* drivers? The ones who aren't as careful as you? See, it's that imperfect world again.

I'll tell you what. Why not invite Debbie to our house

for next weekend? I'll do my best to give you lots of space and running room. Okay?

> I love you,
> Mom

Dear Jennifer,

This is your mom!

How is my little sweetie tonight?

Did you know that I love you so much? Even when you are "crummy" in the morning about what shoes you are going to put on or how terrible your hair looks!!!

Your little face brings me so much joy!

Tomorrow we are going to the auction and we'll have lots of fun. You can wear ANYTHING you want.

So, my little one, take care and sleep well tonight. I love you.

> Love,
> Mom

Darling Girl,

Sure, I know you're only eleven years old, but I'll tell you what—the help you gave me today as I gave a baby shower for Julie sure made everyone (including me) think you're at least twenty-seven years old!

Thank you not only for whipping up Grandma's straw-berry-and-sour-cream Jell-O and for making and baking the brownies, but also for appointing yourself to entertain Julie's little baby so Julie could enjoy the food, fun, and gifts.

Good night, sweetie. Thank you for everything you did to make the shower a big success. (Did you notice? No one wanted to leave!)

You are truly a Wonder Woman!

I love you,
Mom

My dear Son,

I've been thinking about your high-school exams this week. They can sure be rough. (I always froze up on tests and could hardly remember my name, much less any an-swers.)

I just wanted to say that I believe you can get through this week with flying colors. You've studied hard all year long, kept up with your homework, and accepted all that goes with being a senior, *plus* worked at your job at the supermarket.

I also believe you'll do your very best in each exam because you know that while getting an A is great, an-swering questions to the best of your knowledge is more important.

Besides that, you and your sister's exams are on the top

of my prayer list this week. That should count for something. Don't you agree?

Lovingly,
Mom

My dearest Daughter,

   I know by that slightly frantic look in your eyes the thought of exams this week is scaring you silly! (They scared me, too!)

   But I want you to remember something and keep it right up there in your frontal lobes: This has been a *great* year of high school for you because of your teachers, the new friends you've made, and your willingness to try to do your best work.

   I love you, I believe in you, and I expect wonderful things from your efforts!

   And, as I told your brother, the word *exams* is on the top of my prayer list . . . and you know what that means!

   I know you can do it, honey.

My love and prayer support,
Mom

Special Words
of Hope

~

My dear Reader,

To give hope to someone in despair is one of life's noblest deeds. And strangely enough, we who have come close to losing our hope can be of great help to others who are watching their own hope fade into oblivion.

All I usually have to do when I write a note of hope to another soul is to sit back and recall my past. What was it that someone said or did for me when my hope was at ebb tide and I felt it slipping silently away? Who or what revived my dying spirits and gently renewed my zest for life again?

From personal experience I can testify that often hope comes back into our souls from friends' simply spoken words, from gentle hugs or caring touches, or most of all, from one insightful line written in a note that reaches beyond our pain and brings up a wonderful surging of hope within us.

Keep in mind that when people believe, think, or feel that all hope has finally vanished, that's the moment they surrender. They give up. They see absolutely no logical reason on earth to go on living. And without some measure of hope residing in them, they lie at death's door. I know the truth of this. Been there. Done that.

So it is then, at this strategic moment in life, that a few kind actions or words from us can sustain and encourage the soul until hope returns to the heart, making it strong enough to stand on its own two feet again.

Is writing a note of hope a noble deed? Yes . . . for sure.

Love,
Joyce

Dear Peg and John,

I can scarcely imagine what you have been through or what you must be feeling right now.

I'm anxiously awaiting the day when you'll find yourself *beyond* a crisis for a little while. No doubt that seems light-years and planets away right now, but we are all hanging in there for both of you.

One other thought: I believe that God is using you *right now* and even preparing you for service in the future. You are not on a dark closet shelf awaiting a trip to the

Goodwill resale store. Indeed not! You are actually being groomed and molded in the very palm of the Master's hand.

I also believe that when God sees that we are out in the frozen wasteland of despair, he hovers over us, thaws us, and breathes new hope into our collapsing lungs. Then he covers us with his warm blanket of comfort, acceptance, and unconditional love.

Soon, very soon, new life and vitality will spring forth within you two. Then a few things will make some sense, and other things will fall into place. You'll feel as if you have some semblance of normality. Notice I didn't say you'll feel things are *ordinary*; I said you'd feel they are fairly *normal.*

God's grace, his love, and especially his hope are never ordinary. They are extraordinary—like the two of you.

God really did come to give us life—abundant, over-flowing!

I'm with you as we trust God with these awful times. He is able . . .

My love and prayers,

Dearest Roseanne,

Wish I could just drop in for a face-to-face visit. I can see us now, sitting outside on your deck watching the sun sink over those western hilltops and taking in all the beauty.

My heart is focusing on that scene, and I cling to the remembered hope and the peace I feel whenever I'm with you.

Also the memory reminds me that I want to say, on paper, a few things like these:

- When I see your kids, I can tell how much they reflect your guidance and nurturing! Woman, you did something very right!
- When I recall the laugh lines around your eyes, I really see only lifelines reaching out to others and to me.
- And when it comes to being a friend, you're the greatest, and I think, *Oh, my, the world needs more people shaped and fashioned just like you.*

Love,

Dearest Shirley,

This whole week it seemed as if one rotten, unseemly thing after another kept happening. By Thursday evening, I became hopeless. I really believed and felt that nothing would ever be right in my life again. (I'll spare you all the depressing details that led up to this conclusion.)

But somehow in the midst of the depression and sadness that came with the feeling of hopelessness I heard — not aloud or verbally but in a way that my spirit fully understood—God saying, *I'm working this all out, and you'll be pleased when you see what I'm doing.*

I took a few deep breaths, and finally as hope revived me a little, I relaxed.

Please know that right now I'm praying that the Lord will give you this same peace filled with hope—not necessarily the same way he gave it to me, but in a way he knows is best for you.

We are both God's children, so we can depend on him. Remember, too, I shall always be there for you.

Love,

My dear C. J.,

I'm still quite shell-shocked over your phone call. Great balls of fire, what dreadful news!

Let's see if I've got this straight: Your board of directors made the irrevocable decision to fire you? Just like that? What in the world were they thinking?

The "reasons" they gave you are just as bizarre as they are untrue! Everything great and good (and, let's not forget, profitable) that happened during your years there had your handprints all over it! In fact, you were the very best CEO they were ever lucky enough to have!

Hello-o-o-o?!

At any rate, as unfair and unjustified as their action was, still I'm positive that you and your precious family not only will survive but will go on to bigger and better

SPECIAL WORDS OF HOPE

things—mainly because of your tenacity, resilience, and incredible strengths and skills.

I was fired a few years ago, as you know, so I'm familiar with how it feels to have your inner reservoir of hope wiped out in a single day. But I want to tell you about a truth I discovered about God during that brutal experience.

God's track record of taking excellent care of us is always better than our ability to foresee that he will take care of us. And I know that he will take care of us just as well in the *future* as he has done in the *past*.

I'm going to trust the Lord with your well-being, and I'll not be one bit surprised if your next position becomes one of your greatest triumphs!

I'm on your side!

Love,

My dear Madeline,

It's true that no one knows what it's like to walk in another's shoes, but because I'm very familiar with what you're going through, I think our feet must be very close to the same size.

I know, too, that as a Bible study teacher, you are more aware of the healing, hope-giving power of the Scriptures than anybody else around. But I'm writing this one passage down for you because not too long ago these words richly comforted me and restored some measure of hope to my soul. May they do the same or more for your shattered heart.

> Praise be to the LORD,
>> for he showed his wonderful love to me
>> when I was in a besieged city.
> In my alarm I said,
>> "I am cut off from your sight!"
> Yet you heard my cry for mercy
>> when I called for your help (Ps. 31:21–22
> NIV).

God does hear our cries for mercy and for help. In fact, he's listening right now and with his great love is coming to our rescue.

My love,

Dear Joyce,

Today I clearly heard the sad voice of depression in you, and then your words further confirmed the darkness of your despair.

You are running quite low on hope, aren't you?

Oh, dear one, I wish I could give you a large cup of hope . . . or better yet, I'd love to be able to hook you up to an IV bag of hope and wait with you as it slowly drips and seeps into every part of your suffering soul.

Unfortunately, hope is not an easily packaged commodity that one just gets and then gives to another. Hope is an invisible substance; it can only be seen and felt by the heart.

So while I can't rush out and buy you a truckload or even a thimbleful of hope, I *can* do a couple of things:

I can lend you my hope . . . presently I have a good supply of it for you.

I can nurture and massage the little bit of hope that is still alive in you at this moment. And perhaps you'll feel it fluttering inside you.

A friend said the other day, "Hope is the very last thing one clings to before he or she gives up the battle." I know you're weary of war and just want to go home . . . I don't blame you. But as long as you have even a little dab of hope, you won't give up or give in.

However, if you do feel that hope is ebbing away and you know you are losing every drop, please, please call me *before* you do anything. Okay? You and your fragile hopes are safe with me. I'm a phone call away.

I hold you in my heart and pray God revives your spirit and pours his hope into your soul.

My love,

My dear Suzie,

Did you know your name is at the top—the very top—of my daily prayer list? Well, it is!

I thought you might like to eavesdrop, so to speak, on my prayer for you. Here it is.

> Dear Lord, it's good to know that you are
> aware of every fact, jot, and tittle concerning
> the very difficult decision Suzie is facing today.
> Please help her to think and do exactly what
> you know is absolutely the best for her.
> And, Lord, when you do answer her, as I
> know you will, could you include some things
> from her "Heart's Desire" list? You know, some
> of the things Suzie would dearly love to have or
> love to do.
> I really think she deserves it!
> So I thank you, God—in advance.

Suzie, after praying this, I reread the whole Thirty-seventh Psalm, especially the part about us delighting ourselves in the Lord and him giving us the desires of our hearts!

As you can tell, you are very much on my mind these days. Let me know how God is answering.

Love,

Dearest Linda,

As I thought about the situation you're going through right now and how you're bound to be worried about the future (a friend of mine calls this suffering *anticipatory anxiety*), I glanced at the hymnal before me.

The third stanza of the old and sometimes overworked "Amazing Grace" sort of sprang off the page, and I thought, *I'll have to send that to Linda.* So here it is.

> Through many dangers, toils and snares
> I have already come;
> 'Tis grace hath brought me safe thus far
> And grace will lead me home.

We *can* trust that beautiful grace of God to be with us always and to bring us safely home.

Amazing grace.

Love,

Dear Beverly,

May God pitch his tent of mercy over the scorched places in your soul.

That's my prayer for you these days, dear one, and I'll keep on praying for as long as it takes to get you out of the "burn unit" and back into the sunshine again.

My love,

My dearest Friend,

I know you are holding the shattered remains of your marriage in your trembling hands. I pray you will patiently give God a chance to bind up your brokenness creatively.

And in the meantime . . . may I help you to pick up the pieces? I'm here for you—only a phone call away.

You are loved,

Dear one,

I clearly remember when I was drowning in the sea of my despair. But even more, I remember that it was you who came to my rescue and pulled me to safety.

Now it's my turn. Can I give *you* a hand?

I'm ready in a moment's notice, and my boat is seaworthy!

My love,

Dearest Crista,

Let me meet you at the corner of Broken and Shattered Streets.

Let me remind you how God uses broken things. Like Gideon's broken pitchers, a woman's broken alabaster jar, and of course, Jesus' broken body.

SPECIAL WORDS OF HOPE

Then let me tell you about the ways God can bring life to your broken heart. He can, you know.

You are precious—especially in your brokenness, because you are a child of the King—a God who loves and uses broken things.

My love,

My dear Billy,

I was thinking about you, your talents, and your musical career.

Show business! What a complex, frustrating, and perplexing world that is!

But you *are* going to make it. I suspect you're stronger than you believe, and that you'll endure longer than you ever thought possible!

You remember the song "Edelweiss" from *The Sound of Music*? Well, I've been fascinated with the fact that the little white flower edelweiss grows only in the rockiest of crags, high up in the Swiss and Bavarian Alps.

That tiny flower won't bloom in good loam soil or in the warm sunshine, even if watered by gentle spring rains. Oh, no. It blooms from the barest windswept mountain crevices it can find.

You're like that edelweiss, Billy. You are beautifully talented, and you can bloom even under the severest of conditions. Perhaps like that flower you grow *best* during the harshest realities of life!

Besides, you know that you can trust God with the timing of your blooming. You are learning to accept the harshness of this mountain soil because you also know that someday you shall bloom . . . and you'll be spectacular!

Hope this is a great blooming day for you!

My love,

My dear Carol,

When is pain at its very worst?

When does loneliness gather its greatest momentum?

When are fears and doubts the strongest?

In the middle of the night, that's when!

So, that's when I pray for you! I can't sleep either, so I figure praying for you is the best possible use of my time.

You are loved,

My dearest Teresa,

I know, dear one, that you are struggling with some very difficult relationships and circumstances presently. I also know that at times I've contributed to some conflicts, but you know my heart, and I've asked your forgiveness.

But I'm guessing that probably by now your discouragement level has sunk into ever-deepening depression.

In a number of ways, I'm familiar with the helpless

feeling and the sense of hopelessness that often accompany the sadness and depression of our lives.

Victor Hugo wrote, "The word which God has written on the brow of every man is *Hope*."

But sometimes our brows are too furrowed and lined with fears and anxieties for us to make out the word *hope* on them.

Today as I was holding you up in my prayers, Paul's words to the church in Rome came to mind. I felt an urge to put them down on this paper for you.

> May the God of hope fill you with all joy and peace as you trust in him, so that you may overflow with hope by the power of the Holy Spirit (Rom. 15:13 NIV).

Teresa-honey, I can just feel our God of hope pouring his joy and peace over you. And I must believe that in spite of the struggle you're in, you *will* overflow with his hope! And soon!

My love,

Special Reminders

My dear Reader,

Tucked away in the back of my big favorite cookbook is a collection of papers. It contains a brief record of special dinners—the date, menu, and the names of family and friends who ate at my table.

Over the years that record has been a wonderful memory jogger, reminding me of both the food and fellowship and saving me from duplicating the menu with the same guests.

The following pages are designed to help you keep your own records. There are two kinds of pages. The first page, "I Should Write To," will help you to remember to jot down the names of people to whom you really need to write. The second page, "I Wrote To," will remind you of not only *who* you wrote to but *what* you wrote about. Plus, there is a column for you to include the page numbers of letters in this book that gave you help or ideas.

It is my hope that after you've kept this log for even a

short length of time, you will reread your own records, recall the names, dates, and events, and find that these pages will bring you a large measure of quiet and reflective pleasure . . . as I'm sure your letters will have done to the ones you wrote to!

Love,

Joyce

I Should Write To . . .

NAME	WHEN	ABOUT

I Wrote To . . .

NAME	DATE	ABOUT	I USED IDEA FROM PAGE #

I Should Write To . . .

NAME	WHEN	ABOUT

I Wrote To . . .

NAME	DATE	ABOUT	I USED IDEA FROM PAGE #